THE ETERNAL JOURNEY

THE SEARCH OF ULTIMATE TRUTH OF LIFE

DR. MAYANK MURARI

Made with ♥ on the Notion Press Platform
www.notionpress.com

Submission

this soul has to be attained only by truth and by perfect knowledge.

Mundakopanishad 3. 1.5

Through *avidya* they go beyond death and through learning they attain immortality...
through the unborn they transcend death and by birth they take the taste of immortality.

Ishopanishad 11.14

It is the glory of the Supreme God that turns the wheel of Brahman in this world. We
must know that God's Maheshwar, the Supreme God of all gods. His power is also
supreme and the natural action of that power's knowledge and force is multiple. The One
Supreme God, the occult in all beings, the soul of all beings, omnipresent, absolute,
niraguna, is only the presiding, witness, knower of all actions.

Svetasvetra Upanishad 6.1, 7, 8, 11

Contents

Foreword

Preface

Where is the home of greatness? Generally when we think that someone is great, then in our mind comes his position, his identity, his fame or wealth. Every reason that comes to our mind, which is external. Chinese philosopher Lao Tzu is of the view that the superiority which can be taken away, we cannot call it superior or great.

Excellence is not dependent on any external object or cause. We are the best because we have the power. We are great because we have the position. But these are not all benchmarks of excellence. We become the best because of our inner qualities and powers. Nature itself takes a walk and with it all the living and non-living become functional. Then at one point nature leaves everyone. Now it depends on our effort to rise from that stage whether we want to rise above or want to die as we were born. The development of man at that stage depends on our being conscious and aware of our inner qualities, possibility and opportunity. One does not become a human being by filling a human body. He has to be the best. For this you have to travel. And this journey continues throughout life.

Knowledge is essential for excellence. Knowledge is the way to liberation, but not the knowledge we take from others. The knowledge that comes from within us, manifests from our consciousness. That undoubtedly leads to liberation. How to get that knowledge? The founder of Zoroastrianism was the son of Zarathurst. He called the disciples and said that the final sermon was left to be given. He said the last sentence - Beware of Zarathustra. The disciples asked what does this mean? Then he said, ``Do not hold me, otherwise you will be deprived of true knowledge, which can be born from within you. The same thing has been said in another way in our poem – *Ekam Satya Vipraah Bahudha Vadanti*. Truth is one but it has many names and one has to wake up to find it. One has to walk through life by staying alert. No outside knowledge can satisfy us.

In my journey of life so far, I have learned that with every moment of transformation comes the elements of curiosity, change and inspiration.

The events associated with each moment can play an important role in the transformation of our lives. This conversion can happen in an instant or can be the result of long-lasting practice. It may take one birth or many births. But in the end one has to make efforts for self- realization. Under the guidance of Acharya Alar Kalam, Mahatma Buddha self-realized many horizons of wisdom. Then the Guru asked him to lead the monk community. Mahatma Buddha said that please accept my thanks for the teaching you gave me by keeping me with you, but Siddhartha's goal is not to become the leader of any sect, but to find the path of true liberation.

Being the best in life is not easy. To reach the summit in human life, one has to travel on foot. The outer journey in which countless truths are found and the inner journey in which life has to be given direction on the basis of those truths. The life of Shri Ram is the best example of Purusholam's journey (Journey of greatness) for us. Shri Ram himself is an incarnation of Vishnu. The best state of India is the prince of Ayodhya. For them, everything is a simple matter. Despite this, he travelled the country through pilgrimage in the 15th year with permission from Dasharatha. See, know and understand the whole country. Discovered the cultural soul of India. After these journeys they come back, then they become available to inner conscience, dispassion arises in them. Then Rama contemplates like a logical scientist, where he reaches the pinnacle of spirituality through science. Before Shrimad Bhagavad Gita, Yogavashistha is such a great book of brainstorming. After this he got the guidance of great sages of India like Vashishta, Vishwamitra, Gautam, Bharadwaj, Kanva, Parashurama, Agastya, Atri in different stages of his life. Then a whole society with Rama comes alive as a partner in the vast process of cultural transformation.

The way Shri Ram made Purushottam's padyatra (Journey of greatness) easy on the ground of his thoughts and wisdom, Shri Krishna has to reveal the Vishwaroop in the Gita for that solution. It is narrated that after the decision to send with Vishwamitra, Dashrathji called Shri Ram and asked why he is indifferent to all the work nowadays. Rama says that whatever a man does in life is ultimately of momentary consequences and leads to death. Some place in life.

This is not an achievement. All the actions of this momentary life are full of contradictions, discrepancies and contradictions. Wealth, fame, power and position all have their own contradictions in life. Why would any rational being want to be associated with these momentary pleasures? Nachiketa raises some such questions, Arjuna raises doubts in the battlefield of Mahabharata and Tathagata also has to contend with bitter truth in this age. But how does one become Purushottama (greatness)? For this, there is a need to travel within the life of Shri Ram. How? In Yoga Vashistha, Brahmarshi says that neither the mind attains peace by engaging in the affairs of the world nor is it separated from it. But one who separates from these two conditions and looks at life with thought and discretion, becomes entitled to the philosophy of Brahman Satya.

There are two places of pilgrimage to the summit. One, the manifestation of oneself with fundamental ideas on the basis of scientific consciousness, and second, the entry into spirituality with thought and discernment. Watch the life of Ram carefully. He never presented himself as an avatar, even as Purushottam (Journey of greatness). Always walk like a common human standing in the midst of the complexities of life, maintain an equal relationship with ordinary people. They substantiate everything and action on the ground of compatibility with society and justification for justice. He is an avatar, but takes one step carefully. There's no rush. Gives complete original thought of Purushottam's padyatra (Journey of greatness), always keeps the option of leaving Purushottam in front of the society. They tell us that the journey of Purushottam (greatness) lies in assimilating the truth of our life.

Life is a conscious system in which there is not only inertia but also consciousness. He is in motion. Life has its own philosophy. Some eternal sutras of this philosophy tell the truth of our life, which become helpful in our journey to Purushottama (greatness). The path of Purushottam is that which is pleasant and beneficial for the vast human society. Solve the mysteries of life and ascend to the Divinity. The search for truth is done in a new way in every age. Rama in Maryada, Krishna in Karma, Buddha in compassion, Mahavira in non-violence, Shankaracharya in Advaita, Ramakrishna in Bhakti and Gandhi in Truth. All the old discoveries show a way, for our foot journey, to reach the truth of our era.

We create the reality of life only by weaving, chasing and applying our thoughts, fantasies and dreams. If we really look, we are nothing but our dreams, our vision and our thoughts. The journey to the summit is to connect each of your walks to perfection. All creation is a book for us, and its various dimensions are different pages of that book. The journey to the summit is not possible by any one path or by one education. The more we read this nature, and understand the components of this universe, our journey will easily reach Purushottam.

Dr. Mayank Murari
Ranchi, Jharkhand.
Email- Murari.mayank@gmail.com
Mo. 9934320630/ 9308270103

Acknowledgements

In the memory of Mai (Mother), Sunita Devi

CHAPTER ONE

Dr. Mayank Murari

The only one, he. Omkar is the name of the doer; the guy has no need of fear. It is self-proclaimed, ionised, timeless, and without malice. He means that God, who goes by the name Sat, is the name of existence.

Guru Nanak Dev Ji

Finding the light that is inside will dispel the darkness of life

There is a story related to Mahatma Buddha. He had a great disciple, Anand. He stayed with Buddha for forty years in a row, asked for alms, slept together, ate and took advantage of the discourses. He originally lived as the shadow of Buddha. There was a light of enlightenment in Anand's life for forty whole years. When Mahatma Buddha started walking on the journey of death, Anand started crying. He told Buddha- Now darkness will prevail in our life. Then Mahatma Buddha gave the last message - Ananda! How many times have I been with you? Be your own lamp. You don't listen. That's why I have to cry.

Our problem is that we do not listen to ourselves and do not listen to the sages. That's why there is darkness in our life. This darkness will not end with a garland of lamps. Whether it is an electric bulb or the light of a lamp, it is not the light, it is the medium of seeing the object. Deepawali is not a festival to reveal the outer light, but an occasion to revel in the inner light. Light is not experienced from the outside world. Maharishi Aurobindo explains this situation by saying that when looking inside, it is known that what is seen outside is not light but darkness.

There is no life outside. The sages of the Upanishads say that we know one sun, but such infinite suns are illumined in this universe. But we call it the star of the sky, which is much bigger than our Sun. Therefore he prays that you take us beyond the darkness, beyond the light, so that the eternal truth may be seen. There is a kingdom of Tama within us. There is a dwelling of darkness. It does not fade away from outside light. The truth is that the more light we have outside, the more our darkness becomes clearer.

Einstein said one thing - when I started the search for science, I used to think that if not today or tomorrow, everything will be known. But after knowing everything, it would come to know that what remains to be known is so much that even comparison is impossible. Before dying Einstein said that I am dying like a mystic. While he himself was a great scientist. Eddington, another Western scientist, has written in his memoirs that when I began to think, I thought the world was a thing, but now I can say that this world appears to be more and more an idea than an object. Therefore, it is better to illuminate our thoughts, our vision with light than to illuminate the world with light.

The sages say that O Lord! Take me from darkness to light. It implies that there is absence of light in our life and hence the existence of darkness. Darkness is just a lack. There is no position and no one is its power. The person does not understand this and talks of light. We cannot remove the darkness, if it were, we would have scattered it like garbage on the road. It is simple that we do not have knowledge of light. Our journey is still limited to darkness, lack and its manifestation.

We remember that in our childhood we used to pray: - Follow the lighted path, O inner world of ours! We talk about understanding. We talk about that knowledge in prayer, after attaining which light always resides in life. May every moment of life be Deepawali, illuminated with light. For this there is no need to light a lamp or make a person good, but he needs to live life with inner nature. There is no effort but the need to simplify the smooth flow. To be comfortable means to be innocent. Everything is comfortable in this world. Trees are comfortable, animals and birds are comfortable. Only humans are uncomfortable.

Where does discomfort come from? It comes when we try to show what we are not. Nowadays Diwali has become a celebration of the discovery of this uneasy light. There is less light in life, but we try to light up the house and surroundings with such a lamp that everything just becomes beautiful. Knowledge is less but effort is made to become a scholar. A person will be comfortable only when he leaves the journey of ego.

We have never seen light, but always talk of light. We have only seen illuminated things. When it is dark, nothing is visible. Similarly, when the sunlight comes into the world, we see trees, fields, forests, fire, rivers, people, food etc. It is not light, it is an illuminated object. That is why in the

Upanishads there is talk of the journey of truth after light and immortality after truth. This means. Towards this Mahatma Buddha points out that go inside and look, the light is the light. That is the truth. The whole creation is dependent on light, truth and immortality. It is the fault of our vision that we see darkness, untruth and death. But its realization is not possible with lamps, tube light or sunlight. For this you have to travel inside. Self-realization has to be done. Only then our life will be illuminated by eternal light.

Agnimile Purohitam Yagyasya Devam Ritvijam. Hotaram Ratnadhattam. That is, Agnimeele (worship God in the form of light), Purohitam Yagyasya Devam (He is the oriented, the goal of sadhana) Ritvijam hotaram (the motivator manifests through continuous sadhana) Ratnadhattam (the master of all opulences). That is, let us worship the God of light. That is the orientation, the goal of sadhana. He is the master of all the opulence which manifest through continuous sadhana.

Rigveda - First Sukta

The beginning of the infinite journey starts from the inner-self

If you want to make life auspicious and beautiful, then you have to make yourself an image of goodness. There are many forms of goodness. In every movement and action that makes sense, there is hidden goodness. Yet we consider ourselves imperfect. Seek the good for the sake of perfection. But we do not become the perfect model of goodness. Where can I get the knowledge of goodness? Where is the truth? It shakes us for the rest of our lives. It gives a feeling of scarcity.

It is not necessary that goodness should be in a book, in a person or in any teaching and learning. It is in every particle and every moment. It is also incorporated into a small particle, which initially converged with the mountain. Later, when the mountain broke, it separated in the form of a rough and sharp stone. He first lay at the foot of the mountain, then the stream of water carried him down the drain, from the drain to the small river and then to the big river. He kept rolling, rolling while moving under the water and then became a shining *Shaligram* and was enshrined in the temple. Once the sand made of the same stone became the basis of the house. Pandit Jawaharlal Nehru, the first Prime Minister of India, mentioned in a series of letters that this earth is a book. A small obstacle can tell us many things; so many other things that are around us can tell us so many more!

The world is an open book. The visible form, element or word in it on the various pages of that book. We don't read it. If we come to read a river, a mountain, a temple, a forest, a nature, a word, then a stream of good will flow out of it. Nature is open before our eyes, if we learn to read and understand it, then many beautiful stories will be made. If you want to find good, you have to walk. The Upanishads say – *Charaiveti, Charaiveti* means keep going. Life is the name of going on.

The meaning of life is to be in motion. If the speed is there, then everything is fine. Otherwise, if you stop somewhere, then nothing will stop for us. Everything in this universe is dynamic. Everyone is working towards their desired goal. Mobility is based on wisdom. Where to find these ideas? Where can I find these good things? It is a matter related to our vision, thinking and curiosity. One has to seek for the good, question oneself and stand by the truth.

Goodness is everywhere, every moment. If we search with pride, we will find it. Everything or element will manifest itself. If we are filled with enough compassion, then each element of creation will reveal its secret. We rarely do research or research ourselves. Hence less is known. On the other hand God is working through us. So he created many models of goodness and beauty. He created objects or substances like flowers, trees, rivers, mountains, sun, stars to make the universe beautiful and alive. Composed words like travel, prayer, greeting, struggle, time, place. There is goodness inherent in every visible or existent substance, word, feeling, thing or situation. When we are calm, full of compassion, we can find books in flowing springs, teachings in stones, mind in trees, soil or plants in the knowledge of healing.

If goodness is our goal, it will be achieved. Lord Rama found it with dignity, Sri Krishna with yoga, Mahatma Buddha with compassion, Mahavira by non-violence, Socrates with truthfulness, Vivekananda through service to guide the good. Dr. George Washington Carver was an American agricultural scientist who developed new products from peanuts, sweet potatoes and soybeans. His agricultural discovery revolutionized the agricultural economy of South America. He says that this is the creation workshop. There is nothing in life that I have desired and God has not suggested an easy way for that. He talked to groundnut and shankarkand and conducted 300 and 150 new experiments respectively. They say when I talk to little flowers and peanuts, they keep their secrets in front of me.

Where do we think the good is? What can inspire? A person asked God that Lord! Tell us why this universe was created. God replied that you are asking a bigger question than your mental capacity. Then the person said that it is good to tell why man was created? God said that the question is still big. Limit it. Then the person asked why this peanut was made? God said – that is right, but the answer is also infinite. What do you want to know about peanuts? Then the person said that I can make milk from peanuts? God said - what kind of milk! Jersey milk, plain, condensed or whatever. Then God taught that person the art of making different types of milk and other products from peanuts.

The Chinese philosopher Lao Tzu said, "Look at what you can't see, listen to what you can't hear, and try to go where you can't reach." If you want to achieve the good in life or to travel towards the truth, then you have to surrender. Only then will you be able to accept, communicate and understand. The goodness emanating from the various sources and elements of life, which is everywhere. Is contained in every particle and moment.

Remember, my eldest daughter Jia asked a question in childhood? Why is study necessary? I said for knowledge. Then her question was that, why it is necessary to go to school for this? Similarly, for the sake of good, one has to travel within. Inside himself, outside himself. With this time and society. In my search for good, I lost my mother. Then I realized the goodness of tears. The glory of tears is unique. Washes away the biggest trouble in a moment. This enhances the experience. What is river? River means the limitless form of water drop by drop. It is a trip. It is trip of civilization, of tradition, of celebration, of creativity. Life also fills drop by drop. Since the journey of goodness is infinite, so will the search continues. The journey of goodness begins with oneself. After this, its knowledge is realized in the family. The good is constantly embodied in our children, our mothers and fathers, our friends and companions, our co-workers and our daily routine mixed with them. We don't have time to search.

Being infinite, God cannot be confined in any form, human or stone. Yet they appear in all forms. It is right to say that God appears in every human being as well as in great sages, because He is present in all.

Paramahansa Yogananda

The path of dignity in the journey of Purushottam (Greatness).

Gautam's wife, Ahalya is engrossed in the sight of Rama. She is watching. The Brahmaswaroop Ram is lifting from the ground and touching the feet of

Mother Ahalya. With his bountiful Garik Vasan, Ahalya is wiping the dust from the incinerated body. Ahalya thinks O Sparsh! How many forms do you have - how many charms you have! In front of him, pictures of Indra's lust and Gautam's rasa dance on the memory-plate. When Ahalya extends his hand to wipe the dust from his body, Shri Ram stops him. It is said that Goddess, leave it. This dust is the path of my rigorously disciplined journey. From one end of the Aryavarta to the other, I will purify the earth with this austere dust. Establishment of the highest ideal of dignity in life was the goal of Shri Ram's life. Ram's life always connects with the dignity of the individual and his struggle in opposition to the strength and expansion of power and system, then is the vehicle of real development of the society. Seven thousand years ago, this great man challenged Indra and Ravana together. Enjoyment and power. Decorated the dream of the masses, took them along, made co-travels and emerged victorious.

Ram's entire life was spent in confronting the physical culture. When the body and its enjoyment and energy had a central role in society, he made a successful and meaningful effort to change this definition. He replaced the limits of thought and reasoning through Yagya and fire, and through the expansion of scientific materialistic consciousness. It was manifested by the growth and expansion of agricultural civilization, which led to the end of the declining social civilization. The practice of thought and conscience, in which there was a balance of dignity, started from his childhood. When Rama was fifteen years old, a keen interest in pilgrimage developed in his mind. After taking permission from his father, he left for India tour. During his journey, Shri Ram travelled through rivers, forests, ashrams, jungles and the frontier seas and mountains. Traveled in the rivers from Ganga to Jhelum and Chenab and from Kedarnath to Shri Shail, Pushkar etc. He saw the sixty-four places of Vishnu and Shiva and the banks of the four oceans. After such visits, tenderness is born in the life of Shri Ram and prejudices end. After this journey, Shri Ram becomes available to the inner conscience. Vairagya is born in them, then Dasharatha sends them to Vasistha. The dialogue of Shri Ram and Vasistha is recorded in Yogavasistha. It is revealed from this dialogue that Rama always behaves very measuredly like a thoughtful philosopher. In conduct, Shri Ram reveals the self of India through Vivek i.e. Maryada, which he learned as a result of pilgrimage and travel.

The manifestation and fulfilment of the spirit of dispassion through pilgrimage occurs in Yogavasistha. Here Vasistha explains that - neither by putting the mind in the work of the world, there is peace nor by removing the beyond. Whoever sees these two states of mind simultaneously with his contemplation, rises above and becomes entitled to the vision of Brahman truth. In the personality of Rama, the way the matter of thought, discretion and behavioural decorum is in the central role. Because of that, their relation with others is not that of the devotee and God. Bhava has a central role in Bhakti. All the behaviour of Ram is full of thought and conscience. Shri Ram, who is humble and full of respect, gives complete freedom to even the younger one to behave like himself.

Vishwamitra started the tradition of transmutation which Ram was making easy and accessible to all. To make this journey of society and country building meaningful and participatory, he took the support of Vasistha, who was his ideological opponent. One is a state dependent sage and the other Vishwamitra is a social sage. Vasistha prepared the background for the meaningful use of Shri Ram's thought consciousness on the land of Karma, so Vishwamitra helped that thought consciousness to walk successfully on the path of action. As a result of this visit, Vishwamitra was able to participate in transforming a successful social system. It reflects Shri Ram's dispassion and thought that Videha and philosopher like Janaka gives tacit consent on the decision of Shri Ram during his exile. The scholar of jurisprudence, whose curse made Ahalya a stone by Gautama, was turned upside down by Shri Ram. Not only this, Indra, who was a symbol of occultism, also gave a proper answer to him in the marriage mandap of King Janak. Indra, Ravana and the carriers of such materialistic system, misusing the occasion of the dignified banquet given at the time of Shri Ram-Sita's marriage, tested the patience of Shri Ram through abuses, slanders and slanders. This Maryada Bhoj once again served as a stop for the journey of Purushottam with dignity. By testing the eligibility to bear Vishnu's bow, Rama becomes a symbol of judicious destructive power before Parashurama and all the destructive powers. . For this reason, he became a symbol of India's identity, cultural integrity and national consciousness.

In the vast process of cultural transformation, Gautam's philosophy of justice, Bharadwaj's scientific discovery, Atri's ashram system and Agastya's cultural synthesis became instrumental in the vast process of cultural transformation. The contribution of such great sages in the work of awakening the nation through the creation of a single great man in world history is not seen. By limiting social creativity and inner transformation with the foundation of his behaviour and thought, Shri Ram creates a human and dynamic political consciousness, which together shows the functioning of Brahma, Shiva and Vishnu. Rama enters into spirituality through the intensity and subtlety of thought. He always walks in step with life. Because of this, they make easy relations with ordinary people. He tests everything, every action and behaviour on the criterion of social coherence and justice and propriety.

Your inner growth depends on realizing that the only way to find peace and contentment is to stop thinking about yourself. When you understand that the all-time-talking "I" is never satisfied, then your growth begins.

Michael A. singer

Search for divine energy in the night

Night means darkness. It scares me. But darkness teaches us many things apart from light. But who becomes the companion of darkness in life? By looking at the moon, mental power is gained, there is sweetness in life. The darkness that comes in life gets meaning. We believe that auspiciousness begins with Brahmabela. When the sun arrived on the horizon, there was communication of energy in life. This message is universal. This contemplation has considered the importance of half of the life i.e. night as secondary. We spend the night sleeping. If you want to do well, then wait for the morning. But it is not like that. Darkness is not just nothingness. It gives more lessons than light. If you accept this, then the voices of the words will be heard. This will become an effective weapon to remove the problem.

Life is duality. Good and bad. Light and darkness. For this reason, darkness is as important as light. Many things cannot be learned in the light of life. That night it is possible in the dark. We have to accept the darkness. American spiritual leader Barbara Brown Taylor has a book, learning to walk in the Dark, in which she challenges the belief that the dark is intimidating. That's bad. There is a widespread belief that you are in darkness, that is, God does not believe in you. While there is no such a thing. Lord Krishna was born on the Ashtami date of Bhado, Krishna Paksha. It remains the most dark on this date. Darkness is necessary for man to be close to God. It gives the basis of knowing God. Gives invitations. Gautam Buddha enlightened the world by meditating in darkness and solitude.

Taylor writes in his book that mental and physical strength, achievement of goals and true faith can be achieved only in the dark. Darkness teaches us many other things apart from light. Walk slowly in the dark. This gives rise to wisdom and discretion. There is freedom from fear. And then we are close to God. She says that to do this the moon should be made the base.

The time of its rise and set is fixed. Plan with Uday and test when all the light is gone. There is a light even in the darkness. Recognize him

If you want to reveal another horizon of light in life, then you have to make the night a guide. Sitting with the dark it will give light in life. First there is darkness, then comes the light. Life first resides in the mother's womb. The seed first remains asleep inside the ground. Darkness resides there but there is energy, which illuminates life. Makes a seed a tree. Energy and light are two sides of the same coin. The creation of the organism in the mother's womb continues in the dark for nine months. Any great creation happens only in the dark. The creation or creation of every animal, plant or animal goes on in the darkness in the womb of the earth or the mother. Darkness is the time of creation. Sun is needed to bloom. Light is needed for progress, but creation and power accumulation are not possible during the day. Power is lost during the day.

Once Kaka Kalelkar was roaming around to see the condition of the Santals of Jharkhand. Reached a village in the evening. There the conversation started with the people. Slowly the light started to decrease. Uncle said to a householder there that - it is getting dark, it would be good if you bring a lamp! That person of the village started looking at Kaka with surprise and said-Diya? We never use diyas. The sun hid that our business ends. Then the morning broke that we all get busy in our work. Kaka Kalelkar wrote in his memoirs that - this kingdom of darkness in the human settlement? I got very worried. But these people don't feel bad about it. Darkness will definitely come at night. His sorrow should be celebrated, this thing also does not cross the mind of these people. Kaka writes that - I could not even imagine this life without a lamp, who used to speak equally on Indian culture, life and the land of India. After thinking for a while, I felt that, in fact, instead of feeling sorry for these people, I should feel sorry for myself.

Poetry is the purpose of life. Moving from Asuratva to Suratva is poeticism and Upanishad calls it only *Tamaso Ma Jyotirgamaya*. This is the work of awakening a call, so that our word, form, truth, light can be installed in the form of immortality. Humanity resides in natural light, and intimacy resides in natural darkness. This darkness provides an opportunity for contemplation. Darkness is a place of introspection. When we talk about moving towards the light, it means that by erasing the inner Tama and Kalush, the soul should illuminate itself with light. Darkness serves as nourishment to illuminate with this self-light. Even a person who stays under the light in the house all night has to cover himself with darkness to sleep and meditate. Even during the day the light is dimmed for sleep and meditation to reveal the inner light. As much as sleep contributes to removing a person's fatigue, so does the darkness in whose lap a person sleeps peacefully.

That's why it is said to search for energy in the dark. If we accumulate energy, then life will be filled with light. The divine secret is hidden in the darkness. Perhaps for this reason Sandhibela (Dusk time) was said to be the appropriate time for meditation. When there is neither darkness nor light. In meditation the person is always under the protection of energy. That's why in the night time, when nature is calm, we are near to God. Man got the company of God in the dark. Be it Muhammad or Saint Francis or any Hindu saint. All the Vibhutis (great saints) meditated in the caves of the mountains, and found the light. It is said that God met Abraham at night. The Ten Commandments were given to Moses in the darkness on Mount Sinai. The resurrection of Jesus Christ took place in the dark, Shri Krishna came to this earth in the dark. All religions searched for God in the dark. Whether it is prayer or meditation, darkness is considered suitable for this. God is closer to us in the void of darkness. His energy flows unhindered on us.

Night is our friend. It removes the tiredness of the day. Gives the sweetness of sleep to the tears of sorrow. The pain gets ointment only at night. There are a thousand stories of the night. He hides our sorrows in the dark. The day runs away from us, but it is the night that stays with us. It stops. With the beautiful moon, with the fragrance of the queen of the night, with the earth covered with harsingar (One type of flower). Along with the humming of crickets and the glow of fireflies, she gives a voice – The night is a friend, the lamps have been lit. It is only in the night, in which the lamps in the form of the soul can be illuminated. Where is the time of day? If there is time, then where is the peace? If it is night, then there is peace. And if there is peace then there is peace. There is a way. When we consider all of life, it appears that the darkness of the world and the ignorance of the heart are not two different things - they are one. Darkness also has as much universal and universal power as light has.

As a child, I used to look forward to these nights. Then the whole family used to be together. Mother used to live with her. Grandma's stories used to show the way. A beam of power through which they used to search for the pole star among the stars. Used to search for Mars and Venus. Through him the children used to listen to the stories of Dhruv and Guru Brihaspati. Used to study then there was a light in the night in which we used to make our relation. This relationship continues even today. In a slightly modified form. Then they used to know the way and direction on the pretext of Dhruvatara. Today we search for our relatives in those stars. They make Chanda their maternal uncle, Taare their ancestors i.e. grandfather, maternal grandfather, brothers. This is what was taught and told in childhood. Only those who leave this world become stars. Searching for the mother among the stars in the dark, when one falls asleep, it is the wonder of the night itself. Night is as important in life as air and water. It gives dimension to life. To live of a belief just like when the moon peeps through the clouds in a dark and rainy night.

Only after knowing oneself, a person is able to do the right thing with all his knowledge and thinking. He feels unity around him. After this whatever he does is supreme and its results are also unlimited. Both his will and his goal are included in the divine providence.

Maharishi Arvind

Prosperity is not all about happiness

In the current era of globalization, the secondary of the social and cultural aspect is the sign of our crisis. In the market-driven era, there is only one goal – maximum attainment of wealth and abundance of happiness. The foundation of the society, the concern with the family and the rites of passage is missing. This is also the main reason for the downfall of the society. Now there is no question, because society itself has become the question.

In such a situation, one remembers the question of Maitreyi, the sage wife of the Upanishad period. Maitreyi had asked her husband Yajnavalkya that *kathan ten amrita syam*? That is, if this whole earth full of wealth becomes mine, will I become immortal by that? This quote is from *Vridaranyak Upanishad*. When the sage Yajnavalkya got bored of worldly life, he proposed to divide the property between his two wives Maitreyi and Katyayani. Maitreyi then asked this question? In the current market world, everything i.e. person, relationship, time etc. has become value based. That's why the economical young generation and the family that protects it are alienated from their heritage. It is different from the concern of the society, which used to connect the person with the society, the state and their institutions on the basis of love, peace, and compassion. Used to move forward.

Globalization has made the life of an individual meaningless. Everyone is running for material happiness, convenience and prosperity. At the inner level, a voice comes from the soul – we are doing wrong. Still running after money. Deceit, illusion. Nothing is left. This feeling leaves when death is near. Then there is knowledge. The race for money is futile. Nothing works. Politicians, bureaucrats are in jail. Also suffering from many incurable diseases. Where is the money useful? What he earned, he lost in this life. Along with that money, he also lost his fame and reputation.

If only money was everything. Position would have been the goal of life. So Mahatma Buddha would have left the kingdom? He himself says in *Dhammapada* that even if there is rain of money, man's work does not satisfy him. All work (desires or lusts) is tasteless and painful. The *Chakravarti Rajpada* (Renowned Kingship) for which Chandragupta kept on struggling throughout his life. Left everything at the last moment. Rajpad, respect and prestige. Even the clothes of your body. He remained naked for many years. Money is important. Actually money in itself is not a bad thing. The real issue is your attitude towards it. It is necessary for life, but should every movement of life be limited only around money! Don't we need love, relationships, emotions, positive energy and creative dreams! How will you measure the value of these things with money? But see the irony of being judged. Money has become the only yardstick to test everything. Things like science, technology, which can create great things for humanity, are also being used only for material development.

If you want freedom from this, you have to have the courage to ask questions like Maitreyi. Will have to show resolve like Nachiketa. It has to be known from the guide of the society – *Yenahan Namrita Syam Ki Mahan Ten Kuryam?* What is the auspicious goal of life? What is the secret of immortality? This question is not happening from India. The West is asking this question, albeit in a low tone. Via Bill Gates and Baren Buffett. For this one has to understand the meaning of success. What is the index of success? Everyone wants to be successful, but the result of success is- worries, stress, diabetes, blood pressure, ulcers, insomnia or fear and worry? There is only one sign of success – a smile on your face. A smile that comes from within, and exhilarate the mind and body. Maybe Because of the money, Alexander came to Asia in the mood of conquering the whole world. So he came to know that the whole world is far away only India is limitless. While returning injured from India, he told his courtiers that when he dies, keep his hand out of the shroud. So that people see that only knowledge and goodness go after death.

Man is the biggest symbol of the divine element, God is looking for this element of his every moment. He also keeps knocking at our door to come. But we ourselves are controlled by our centres of pleasure.

Ramakrishna Paramhansa

God is all the changing world and everything in it

If the solution to all the problems of the world and the balanced and true development of the individual is contained in a single verse, then it is the very first mantra of Ishopanishad. With this Richa it is possible to solve all the personal and social concerns related to sustainable development, environmental protection, pollution free, unemployment, inflation, modern lifestyle. This mantra of the Upanishad shows one the path of ascent to a spiritual path. Leads us towards truth and such a life, where the goal of development and nutrition of the entire universe is achieved with the technique of enjoyment. This mantra begins with Ishavasya. That means everything belongs to God. The complete mantra is-

Om Ishaavasyamidam Sarvam Yatnikach Jagatyam Jagat.

Ten Tyekten Bhunjjitha Ma Gridha: Kasya Sviddhanam.

This verse tells that everything that is in the entire changing world is covered or pervaded by God. We should nurture ourselves with sacrifice and should not covet anyone's money. We live our whole life in this Maya and illusion that this house is mine, this wealth and this fame, this lineage, this position and prestige are mine. Whole life we go round in the illusion of this illusion. The question is whether this birth happens by my will. Will I die by my will? Do we get anger, love, fame, position or children by our will or mind? Probably not. Everything happens through means, nothing has our will. We have nothing. This is the madness between this life and death. To accept as our own, to consider as our own. This house is mine. Let's name it. Of the house, of the person and of the position. When we do not have control over hunger, sleep and mind, then how can anything happen to us? All the feelings, objects and situations in life appear before us from some horizon and go away after some interval. That horizon, that end and that point of origin is God and that which pervades life and creation. Science calls it nature. But when science says nature, then we become powerful. An arrogant person stands up. But when the Upanishads say that He is God, then our ego vanishes. We accept humility. This difference of thinking is also visible in the work and religion of life.

Adiguru Shankaracharya repeatedly says in his famous *Bhajgovindam* that you fool! Leave excessive desire for money. Leaving the name Govind, hold on to the feeling. Indian philosophy talks about connecting and realizing God in this world. The meaning of sacrificial enjoyment is, the one who leaves, he enjoys. One who clings to name, wealth, fame and position? You don't even get the pleasure of bearing his responsibility. When everything belongs to God, there is nothing to hold on to. Whether it is fame or infamy, whether it is happiness or sorrow. And then what to do with greed from other's money? But where does a man under Maya understand this?

Ingersoll, a famous American agnostic, told Swami Vivekananda during the discussion on enjoyment in the talk that I believe in getting the most out of the world. I want to squeeze it dry like an orange because this visible world is a definite thing. After this answer Swami Vivekananda told Ingersoll that Indians also squeeze this earth more than a western man. An Indian knows that he does not die, so he is in no hurry to squeeze it. That's why he takes pleasure in squeezing, enjoyment and feels God. When we can see and understand life without being free from selfish exploitation, then only we will be able to truly enjoy life.

What is this world except the blissful Brahman? And we are on this earth for his enjoyment. We keep the vision of renunciation only in the state of being simple and then only the bliss of Brahman which is included in everything of this earth is visible. Had it not been so, Gandhiji would not have used only one bucket of water from the Ganges at the Sangam for his bath. It is said that when Jawahar Lal Nehru told him that Bapu, this is the Ghat of Sangam and there is no water crisis here, then Gandhiji had said that crores of Indians have a right on this water. I used as much as I had the right. Excessive indulgence is wrong. This is the true joy of life and a holistic vision.

In life, when we leave, relinquish, we do not become empty. But giving up is not just for getting. If this happens then he will be guilty. Then we cannot say ten *tyekten bhunjjitha*. The person who leaves, is always full of freshness, newness, newness, new happiness, new thoughts, conscious knowledge. And the one who is always full, is not ready to be empty or to leave, then he remains deprived. Its parts are found dilapidated. Today, be it the problem of unemployment, or hunger or climate crisis, there is only one reason behind all of them – we are caught. Your stubbornness, your thoughts and your vision. Your possession of other's wealth. Fulfilment of selfishness in wrong way. Always a sense of exploitation. While we have no right to do so.

This society ordinary person made for threes. Here the extraordinary person will always be restless and inconsistent. But this is the person who has given something to the society, has accelerated the development. Has enriched human life.

Calin wilson

Why is there a problem of suffering in this world of God?

Everything is in the hands of the creator, so why does he create sorrow in this world. One answer would be that it appears to be due to our ignorance. Sorrow or happiness or light and darkness. These are dualities. Creation is dual. Nature and man. Shakti and Shiva. The strongest question on this was raised by Savitri's mother. It has been given a detailed form in the epic Savitri composed by Maharishi Arvind. Savitri's mother asks sage Narad - why did we come here? If ecstasy and indescribable peace is our goal, then why all this? If we have to live life, then what is the need of ignorance and tears? Where did sorrow and grief come from? Or did you come just like that? Our life is born with the call of pain. After this, the tax of time and the claim of God have to be paid continuously. Many types of diseases and sorrows keep suppressing our bodies, make us experience bad experiences of torture and finally hand it over to death.

Who forced the immortal soul to take birth? Who gave him the mind to give up his right to immortality? Didn't some Mahamaya create a constellation? Then where is the security of the soul? Making a final attack, she says that perhaps what we perceive as the soul is just a dream and the eternal Brahman is a contemplative fiction. Naradmuni answers that - so what is night, that's why sun is only a dream? But it is not even that much.

Arvind gives a logical explanation to this – where there is ignorance, there will be unhappiness. Happiness and sorrow are born in pairs, but first the birth of sorrow has happened and only after that the birth of happiness is possible. Sorrow is the cube of the gods. The act of breaking the inertia of the individual hurts, awakens the self-conscious and the awakened consciousness then learns to ascend towards the Sun of Light. There is another argument. Our mother earth is still in labour pain. Thousands of years have passed, but till now, except for a single divine soul, such a situation has not come where the whole world can ascend to divinity. This earth is suffering in order to prepare man for the divine life after the pangs of childbirth. But this is a human being, so stubborn and arrogant, who doesn't care about it. He just wants to be lost in his ignorance and material happiness. For the sake of divinity, for the supremacy of this creation and for an enlightened life one is bound to take birth, suffer and die. He has to adopt it. Till now a divine light arrives in different periods, whom he learns, saves, and there he becomes his enemy. He has to cross a river, crucify, shoot an arrow in the leg, exile and give poisoned food. However, the community benefits from this and climbs towards divinity by beating hands and feet. But humanity is not able to succeed in this.

Perhaps it was said that - O human, adopt the rule of sorrow in life. Take support of the infinite power of God, make him your refuge and move towards the ultimate goal. When Shri Krishna gives Kunti, the mother of the Pandavas, an opportunity to ask for something, she says-

Disaster: Santu Ta: Shashwat Tatra Tatra Jagadguru.

Bhavato darshan yat syadapunarbhavdarshanam. (Shrimad Bhagwat 1/8/25)

That is, O Shri Krishna, I want that all these calamities should come again, the cover of sorrows should remain. So that we can praise you, it is possible to see you again and again, because seeing you means going beyond this world, the cycle of birth and death. Mother knows that the material world is full of troubles – *padam padam yad vipadam.*

The stories tell that the prayer of Prithvi Lok forced Savitri to take birth in this mortal world. Savitri was born to rebel against ignorance and mortality. Successfully challenge the gods who had dominion over immortality. Instead of accepting the subjection of the unknown world, pave the way for liberation yourself. So, knowing it, he accepted the suffering.

Shri Krishna came on this earth only to suffer this sorrow and to give a message to the universe. There is a dialogue between Shri Krishna and Rukmini in the epics. Rukmini says - I am jealous not of Radha, but of Mother Devaki. Jealous, of their overall femininity. Krishna says that Devi reveals a truth which the world did not know. Krishna says- Mother Devaki and her son Shri Krishna are the most unfortunate mother and son in the world. Which no people or humans can imagine! The best moment in a woman's life is the joy of motherhood. Mother Devaki had eight sons each, but she could not give milk to any child by hugging her. The birth of every new-born child would fill him with sorrow and fear. Not only is this, for every new born baby, breastfeeding by hugging its mother's breast the biggest pleasure and right. But I was deprived of this natural right also.

Shri Krishna realizes this in the latter half of his life. The question also arises, why didn't you realize earlier? Where did Krishna get time for this with his birth? Life crisis in childhood, and later the responsibility of establishing religion kept him away from this enlightenment. Shri Krishna says- memory-forgetfulness sometimes creates such inaccessible mysteries. Life always remains a formidable problem for the one who can understand more and more of this impassable. Of Shri Krishna Last moments of life. The arrow hit the sole of the foot, the fowler started lamenting. Shri Krishna consoles - you have become the reason for the curse to fructify. Don't keep any burden on your mind. After completing the work for the rest of your life, you too should move upwards. He remembers the curse of Mata Gandhari, the curse of Maharishi Kashyap and the pride and arrogance of his clan and his people.

Where was his fault in this? Krishna contemplates - his life itself proceeded under the shadow of death. After birth, just started walking on knees that Putna aunty reached. After this he saved himself from Shaktasur, Bakasur, Dhenukasur, Kaliyanag etc. Gave the message of fearlessness to the residents of Gokul. But when the time came to leave Gokul, when disaster in the form of Kansa struck his life, no one was with him. Neither the residents of Gokul nor the residents of Mathura. When Lord Krishna left his Gokul, no one went with him. Mother Yashoda is mournful on the visit of God. She looks at Gokulvasi, looks at her family. His heart-rending cry rises-

Jasuda used to be like this again and again.

Is there any one in Braj in our way, please keep Gopal.

Gopal is leaving Braj. The patterns of natural life are leaving us, they are getting separated. No one cares. No effort. there are so many companions in Gokul, there are heroes. Somebody stop that Kanha. No one is left in our interest, is it? Krishna strove for identification with the whole life, association with the whole environment and oneness with the society. But where did the society listen? Had this happened, Mahabharata would not have happened. But it happened. The *Yaduvansh* itself was destroyed. Perhaps this is why Shri Krishna says that although no work is impossible for me and it is not that it is necessary to do any work, but still I work so that the right example can be set in the world. This is the reason why Krishna raised himself when the time came. This power is in me, it is in everyone. This is also because the soul itself becomes a friend when we lift ourselves up and becomes an enemy when we let ourselves down.

When Shri Krishna's great journey takes place, then Kuruvansh finds himself sluggish. Pandavas do not understand any meaning of living. Arjun's own powers start to wane. Once in a dialogue between Shri Krishna and Narad, Munivar raises the question that Yadavshrestha could not attain Godliness. What is the reason of this? So the answer is that-distribution of the uncommon to the common means that Lord Krishna gave a part of his Krishna to his people like Satyabhabha, Balram, Ugrasena, Akrur or Kritavarma. The sanskar and opulence in the form of sanskars which have to be promoted, they got all that easily. Because of this they could not attain all the divinity. There is only one Shri Krishna, who transforms sadness like Arjuna into yoga, then he himself gives direction to the sorrows of his mind. It is not easy to convert depression into yoga or to provide a part of opulence and Krishna element to the common man.

No one else understood this sorrow better than Yudhishthira? Nakula expresses the suffering of 12 years during the exile-

Our family has never left the side of religion. Religion does not set. Nor has any target remained impregnable due to laziness. Then why, my lord! Why do we suffer so much in spite of being so elevated among all beings? The past never leaves the Pandavas. Everyone has their own sorrow. But everyone is forced to live with that sorrow for the rest of their life. Yudhishthira becomes the ruler of India after the Mahabharata war. But even then there is no peace. The author of Mahabharata says at the end- Raising hands, I scream, but no one pays attention. One gets wealth and happiness through religion, then why is religion not followed?

It is difficult to follow the religion. There is sorrow on the path of religion but there is progress. It is human helplessness that takes us down from the moral life. Yudhishthira is the son of Dharma, that's why he keeps on supporting Dharma, but when Arjuna keeps getting Krishna's support, then sadness turns into Yoga, defeat into victory. To understand sorrow, understand happiness? Yaksha asks this question to Yudhishthira, then he puts his past life in front of him. Answers- The one who cooks food in his house, who has no debt and is not exiled, he is happy. Means there is no difference between sorrow and happiness, it is the mood. There is a difference in quantity. Yaksha asks - what is new? Time eats the soul, that's what's new. An interesting question related to the meaning of life arises that what is the highest religion in the world? For this a word is used Anrushanya means compassion. To grieve and feel the pain of others. This is religion. This is life and this is the solution to get rid of sorrow. Because sorrow is there, for the development of life.

Yudhishthira lived every action of life. Not only on the ground of the body. The body has to suffer, so it will suffer whether it is happiness or sorrow. He lived life at the level of the mind and beyond that at the level of the soul. The body is a machine and its actions are mechanical. At the level of the mind, the individual's actions become mental, where the individual becomes one with the actions. But there is another plane on which people like Shri Krishna, Buddha, Savitri, Socrates and Yudhishthira live their lives. This is the plane of the soul. At this level, physical senses and mental activities become secondary. Man goes beyond action. Like Tantra. Every moment God resides in his life, then nature itself is doing its actions. Nature's work and God's religion are involved. With great pleasure

It can be explained simply in this way – each of our activities takes place on three levels. Some morning went out for a walk. Went out for a walk, but remained tied in a chain of countless thoughts. It is on the physical level. The food is in front of you but the taste is not known. This is living on a mechanical level. If a person becomes one with him while taking a walk. Feel the winds, welcome the sights of nature. If the chirping of birds, the rays of the sun, the sound echoing from a distant temple bring sweetness to the mind, then the person is mentally active. Savouring food or a walk with emotion, the process of creating emotion with it, is another level of living life. There is another level apart from this - Tantrik means spiritual. What is this? Like food Upanishads say - *Anna Brahman*. Food is God. How? We take food, but food is a substance, so from where and how is intelligence, sharpness, power, blood and knowledge created from it? Who fills life with juice? In the chirping of birds and in the gust of wind, if the juice of that divine is found in the walk, then where is the sorrow in life? This life is meant to take the journey from the physical to the tantric level. Replace with divinity. Transform life.

The senses bring out the soul of man. Man is searching for happiness and joy in places where he can never find them. Through the ages we have been taught that it is futile and futile. We cannot find happiness here. But we cannot learn.

Swami Vivekananda

God's gravity is to uplift the consciousness

There is a Sufi saying that bettering oneself is the first step towards building a better family, better society and a better country and world. Resolution to improve is the mantra of life. By using it one can take the quality development of human life towards excellence. The journey to this excellence is the basic nature of this universe. Everyone is trying to achieve that excellence with their power. The way we have will power, similarly the gravity of the earth is power. Similarly, there is another power, the Divine Gravitational Energy, which is always attracting the variable and non-living beings and non-living beings of the universe towards excellence.

The earth has its own hidden energy which pulls everything towards itself. This secret power is called the force of gravity. If a fruit falls from a tree or an object falls from a multi-storey, it will come down. Any object that is pulled down by the magnet is not visible, but the result is visible. In the same way,

God also pulls things towards himself. The name of his pulling power is Grace. Grace is what we can call prasad, or grace or attraction. When flowers bloom in plants, they rise up, that is, towards the sky. When consciousness expands in a man, he becomes lighter when he is filled with joy. Consciousness expands in animals and birds and also in humans. When this happens life rises up.

Whenever there is rain of bliss in any conscious entity, there is exuberance in the heart, the body dances, then they blossom like flowers and turn towards the sky. This is the yearning to meet God. When we are awakened, when we attain the state of consciousness, then we get the prasad of God. If there is sweetness and satisfaction in the form of juice, smell, colour and fruit in the petals of flowers, then man becomes overwhelmed by his grace. On the other hand, when we are dilapidated, die or are sad, we fall down, the earth pulls us down and makes us sleep in the mud. Here the offerings of God's love are seen in different forms. He sometimes appears through the smiling flower, the grave mountain, the chilling ocean, the swell wind, the playful bird and the human being full of consciousness.

The great French philosopher Simon Wells has written a book, Grace and Gravity. In spiritual books, it has a place in the great book of the world. They say that just as the earth pulls things towards itself, similarly God also pulls things towards itself. God is always attracting us towards himself. The dreaming consciousness of God first appears in the stones or inert minerals. Then it starts acting as a sensitivity in trees and plants. Here his self-consciousness does not appear. It then emerges as the sentient life of animals and birds. In man the gift of the same God is expressed in the life force and consciousness, the superior intellectual power of reason and discrimination.

God becomes a river to bless with his grace so that those who come close to him can drink nectar in the form of water. Sometimes he becomes a mountain so that he can see the peak of love, he becomes an ocean for the vastness of love. Then the divine love of that God keeps on throbbing in the hearts of infinite souls. When God's offerings increase the fragrance of flowers, the chirping of birds, the embrace of another heart, then His grace is manifested. God's prasad is received from morning till sleep but it is subtle and mysterious. He builds flesh, blood, marrow, bone and brain from the food we eat every day, builds and develops us. But we understand that we are alive because of this food.

The law of attraction is inherent in the universe. When two objects are free to move and they are pulled towards each other, the effect of gravity is visible. The definition of physics states that gravity is the force that exists between two physical bodies and due to which each body pulls the other body towards each other. This rule is universal. All of the earth, the sun and the sky Stars and objects have this force equally. For this reason, the sun, moon, stars and other celestial bodies of the sky revolve around each other cyclically and pull other bodies towards them.

Gravity is not a one-way pull, but a pull between two objects. If we understand the law of gravity properly then only we can understand the prasad or attraction of divine pull properly. In the context of the Moon and the Earth, the power of the Earth is more, so it is able to pull objects towards itself faster. Every two objects have an inherent attraction and desire to attract or attract each other. Everything in life does not happen without conflict, as the fruit falls down from the tree. Similarly, fruits and flowers also come on the tree. Newton's contemporary thinker Ruskin raised the question why he comes. How does it reach the top? Not only this, how does water reach the leaves of five hundred feet above tall trees like bamboo, palm and cedar?

Later scientists discovered that the force that pulls down is the gravitational force while the force that pulls up is the levitation force. In spirituality, sages called this power as Prasad. In the same way God pulls towards Him through the offerings of his infinite consciousness, on the other hand Maya i.e. our ignorance pulls on the other side. Due to foolishness, we ignore the various centres of divine attraction and degrade ourselves. We get trapped in the eternal cycle of birth and death because of our desires and sense pleasures. Keep going away from God. While he continues to bless with his offerings.

Whenever a question needs an answer or solution, stop thinking for a moment and focus on your inner energy field. When you start thinking again, it will be a new and creative thought.

Eckhart tell

Ascending towards the divine man by solving the mysteries of life

There is a story from the life of Mahatma Buddha. Juhi flowers were in bloom all around the *Gandkuti at Rajgir.* Shasta showed those flowers to the monks and said - You see these flowers. Look carefully at these beautiful, blooming and fragrant flowers. There are many secrets hidden in them. You can be such a flower. Flowers bloom in the morning, wither in the evening. Such is the life of man. It has come and will go. Similarly what is the sorrow of our life? The fundamental sorrow of our life is that we want to stop that which will not stop. Which is temporary money. We have taken it for granted. It is a fundamental sorrow that what cannot be done, always wants to adopt it forever.

Actually life is a system. A system that is conscious and dynamic. It keeps on changing continuously. This is also the philosophy of life. The Arya Sutras of eternal truth tell and show us what the meaning of life is limited to. It is not in grasping the fleeting but in knowing the truth. The bottom line is that when everything is about to leave, what is the point of making so many plans? The past is gone, the future will also come and go. The present is in front. Just celebrate it. For this truth, a prince Gautam gave up all the opulence and comforts of the world. wife and son and even the attachment of this body. Leaving everyone, he wandered like a wanderer for years in search of truth. From one teacher to another and finally by merging into himself. One day he attained enlightenment under a Peepal tree and became Mahatma Buddha from Gautama. In the last days of Buddha, Ananda expressed curiosity that *Bhante* would now tell us something about the truth. Pointing to the leaves scattered in the autumn in front of him, the Buddha said, "Anand, I have given you a handful of truths." But like these leaves, innumerable truths are scattered. Is it not true that Socrates drank poison to protect this truth but remained firm on the truth? But today it is said that our truth is greater than your truth.

It is a mirage of truth that in this era once again people have started talking about renunciation and spirituality. It is difficult to say how much of it is spontaneous and how much is pretentious. But there is a story from the life of Buddha. A poor man of Shravasti used to live somehow by plowing. He was extremely sad, like all beings are sad. Buddha's vision came, he became a monk, but his connection with the past does not break. He used to remain sad even after taking Sannyas. After this incident, Mahatma Buddha said in his sermon that man is his master. You are your own pace. It is true that the poor are sad about their poverty and the rich are sad about their richness. Life was spent in richness, didn't know. When the mother died, I came to know that life is between two breaths. Enough. The mother's heartbeat, her pulse, her breathing were all flat on the monitor. Straight. Means there is life only when there is progress and degradation in it. Last time she was giving this message - Son, if life is crooked, it is good. What to worry the emotion of the second made me flashback to a time when life was never straight and flat. Perhaps because of this he had to bear many troubles of life.

Compassion was the truth of Buddha's life. What is the truth of our life? Have we ever tried to think about it? *Tathagat* kept saying throughout his life that what I have, you are also born with the same amount. There is no gap between our intellect, our speech and thinking. The difference is that Buddha pulled the strings of his life so that music could be born. To bring this music to life, we have to find our own truth. Like Ram, It was discovered by Krishna, Buddha Mahavira, Jesus and Nanak. You will find many truths in life, but it will not be your own truth. You have to find your own truth. He will emerge from his own experience. Find a truth. It should be a matter of knowledge. He will be the essence of our thousands of experiences. Modern India has not yet understood that truth cannot be discovered with borrowed knowledge.

If you want to connect with existence with life, then you have to stop and think like Mahatma Buddha. Thirst is within all of us. Some people know this and some don't. Because many are not conscious at all. Milan Kundera wrote a novel called Slowness. In it he asks why the joy of slow motion has been lost. Earlier we used to gaze at the sky comfortably. Love also comes slowly, but people want attention and happiness immediately and instantly. It is in such a situation that Mahatma Buddha asks us that what that truth is. The ascent of divinity while solving the knots of life is the truth. People think that everything is done when they become a monk, when they get initiation, then they become spiritual. This is just the beginning. The journey has to be done inside. Buddha says that - *Tatta hit uttano natho atta hih attano gati. Tasma Sajmayattanam Assam Bhadrav Vanijo.* That means man is his own master. You are your own pace. You yourself become your lamp.

Change is the destiny of nature. Each day is different from the previous day. This change is not meaningless, but every day contains magic within itself. It just needs a little attention. Like days, there is a change in a person too. You are not the same today as you were yesterday, challenges have also changed their form with you.

Paolo Coelho

Our prayer connects man with God

There is a prayer in the 14th verse of *Ishavasya Upanishad-*

The face of Aditya Mandalastha Brahm is covered with a Jyotirmaya Patra. O Pushan, you expose me to Satyadharma to achieve the soul. The ultimate truth of this world is covered by light. Truth will be realized only when the light goes beyond it.

This is the goal of the prayers we pray throughout our lives. Everywhere there is either light or darkness and we cannot go beyond it. Throughout life, we go round the illusion of this duality. Prayer is the last step in the fulfilment of a person's resolution. When we are tired, defeated, we fold our hands. We dedicate ourselves with the voice of prayer. We pray, prayers don't happen. Our action is not correct, because prayer is not an action. These are feelings. Our mood is and in such a situation we become prayerful. The meaning of prayer is that every part of the body starts calling out, every tear gets shaken and there is no desire left. This is the only event in which the person is totally immersed. If it is not so, then the prayer is not fulfilled. It is a living action. In which the ego dissolves as soon as it is engrossed. Humility starts being communicated in life. If there is no humility in life, if we are not able to destroy ourselves, then there is no meaning of prayer. In such a situation, the person folds his hands and says - Lord, now you only do it. Now you only get the journey done. Just your wish

With prayer, a person connects himself with God. Ramakrishna's life is mentioned. A devotee was a guest in the temple of Ramakrishna. He had an idol of child Krishna. He used to bathe him by taking a dip in the Ganges, and used to say in between, tell me how you are? Are you having fun? Swam and swam with him. Plays, walks and also eats together. Vivekananda was surprised. What kind of worship is this? When he told Ramakrishna, his answer was that this is worship. Don't tease him this is the true form of prayer. Sad happens when one bows down in the temple but does not bow down seeing the moon in the sky, the flowers blooming on the earth, the flowing rivers. Nothing happens inside it. Prayer will be meaningful only then, prayer will be fruitful only when we learn to bow before the various forms of this God. If there is love in prayer, then only we will be able to learn to bow down. First God comes, then prayer comes as a result. The experience of God arises within us in the form of prayer in every pore. Prayer is fragrance. Dancing with passion is prayer. Creation by being absorbed is prayer. Kirtan is prayer in devotion.

Prayer begins the day self-confidence ends. As long as there is an ego of self-confidence, prayer does not bear fruit. When the self is big, the divinity will be small. As soon as the self becomes small, the size of divinity starts increasing. The meaning of prayer is not bowing down in front of idols in *Yagya, Havan,* chanting, penance, *bhajan, kirtan* or temple. Lighting a fire, reciting or reciting a mantra is not called prayer. Through these actions, the person is connected to himself. The day when I left myself, and connected my mind with the Lord. He became a prayer. It was said in the hymns of the Indian .Upanishads – now go beyond yourself. Whatever he does is right. Not what I do. Not deeds, not proving merit, not a matter of right. If you become simple, you will become beautiful.

Sometimes it seems to us that there is no answer to our prayers. While God definitely answers our prayers according to the rules made by him. These trees are standing silently. This is his way of praying. Birds sing, this is their prayer. Clouds surround the sky, clouds come on earth in the form of rain. It is a celebration of the earth. Rivers descending from the mountain and running towards the sea all three rivers are praying. The journey to fulfilment is through prayer. This whole existence is praying. Prayer is going on. In the rustle of the leaves of these trees, in the chirping of birds, in the dripping of drops. The whole existence is engrossed in prayer.

We think they should respond to our level in our languages. Paramahansa Yogananda says that he does not speak, lest in doing so he influence the devotee's free will to choose or reject him. The question arises that how does God answer? He responds in the form of fulfilment of desires. This happens when we vibrate through prayers, whose vibrations reach God. Then God wishes that our wish is fulfilled. Sometimes the same God answers our prayers in peace and joy. Sometimes the answer to the question comes to us in a subtle form in the form of intuition.

Prayer gives us emotion. Not the feeling of words but the feeling of the heart. This is not going to be achieved by bowing down in a temple or in any temple. If the desire to ask is implied in the feeling, then it is not a prayer. That praise is demanded. Such prayer is done in the darkness of the night, before the journey, before the examination so that the prayer can be fruitful. This is our wish. Prayers are fulfilled on the day we wish God for eternal life, thank and express gratitude. The day when nothing is visible except the grace of God, that day we will be able to learn how to pray.

The day there is love in the eyes, prayer will be felt in the leaves, in the water of rivers and in the voices of birds and animals. Then we will bow down to the cuckoo's cuckoo and the peacock's dance and will know the journey of prayer in our hearts even in the rain of the clouds and in the sunlight. It is said that his feet are there at every moment and at every place. His signature is on every grain of sand. The basic thing is that our lust is so strong that everything is visible in this world except God's grace and His signature. The day we will be able to say that I have no capability that day transformation will happen. Our words will become feelings.

Ignorance is the root of all calamities. It is ignorance to consider impure things as pure, to consider things that give pain as happiness and to consider mortal things as imperishable. Salvation is possible only after the end of ignorance.

Maharishi Dayanand Saraswati

The infinite journey of life's curiosity in Nachiketa's questions

It is a strange puzzle of life. When the child speaks, tries to explain something, we do not understand. And when we speak it goes beyond the understanding of the child. There is a beautiful story in *Kathopanishad*. Of the dialogue between Nachiketa and his father Vajashrava and Yamraj. The child whom his father could not understand, Yamraj took the test and gave him knowledge like a teacher. Ego does not allow us to be big, simple and intelligent in life. Whether we live in a high position or a low position, in a palace or in a hut, the ego is always with us, as it was with Vajashrava.

The story is that the father is donating such cows, which do not give milk. On this Nachiketa raises the question why its donation? In charity, things that are dear and useful to the society should be given. But this egoistic mind is satisfied by offering bread to the poor, a few rupees to the beggar and sweets to God. Do we not aspire for fame, fame and profit in life on the basis of such deeds? Nachiketa thinks in his mind that I have followed first-class conduct in many and follow middle-class conduct in many. Never behaved below par. Still why does father do this? In the present times, there is a crisis in every sector of the society, instead of simplicity of conduct and high level of determination instead of arrogance.

Nachiketa raises the question that like paddy this human life ripens and falls and is born again like the same. Seasons come and go. The crop grows, the seeds fall, then there are shoots and the crop ripens and the seeds fall. This is a circle. When everything is fleeting and changeable then life should be adapted to the truth. Nachiketa's mind and heart had become fearless because of his love for truth. It is the sense nature that turns man away from truth and dharma. When a man considers himself to be an accumulation of the body and the senses, he revolves in the circle of lust, fear and greed. Today it is stopped on questioning.

Fearless love for truth is looked down upon, then through *Kathopanishad* Nachiketa appears before us as the sun of time. He accepts his father's donation to death and goes to meet Yamraj. Yamraj meets him after waiting for three days and gives three boons in lieu of Nachiketa's steadfastness and steadfastness in truth. Nachiketa's question and Yamraj's answer i.e. boon can become excellent standards of education for today's teacher and disciple. Yamraj tests Nachiketa with every question, and on passing the test gives a proper answer to the question.

If Yamraj is the giver, then someone would beg for all the wealth of the world! Started wishing for heaven and complete prosperity. But how to be an ideal child? It was replaced by Nachiketa in Indian life. He asked for the first boon that my father should calm down and receive me lovingly as a son when I return. The second wants the knowledge of that knowledge in the form of a boon, from which heaven the beauty of is on the palm of man. After this Yamraj gave Nachiketa the knowledge of that Yagya Vidya, after attaining which there is no dearth of opulence with man.

After Nachiketa, Ashtavakra, Mahatma Buddha, Shankaracharya, Kabir why there is lack of innovative and great personalities in Indian life. Swami Vivekananda tells us the answer to this that we allow ourselves to flow in the stream of life like floating wood? Change used to happen in the whole world, it happens but we are unaware and ignorant of it. Nachiketa also had such a situation, but he thinks that longevity is also short, happiness has to wane, life is passing every day, so what would be the benefit of a boon? He questions atma tattva as the third boon. What is the answer to this question - *uttisthat, jagrat, prapya varannibodhat, kshurasya dhara nishita duratyaya, durgam pathaspad kavyo vadanti* (1.3.14). Swami Vivekananda also had this favourite mantra. The poets of the Upanishads are exhorting that attaining knowledge should be the best goal of a man's life. But its path is inaccessible, so go to the scholars and gain knowledge.

Nachiketa's third question opens two layers of the inquiring mind of man. One who is bounded by and entangled in nature. And the second which is part of modern scientific thought. Through these questions, life can be made meaningful and worth living. We forget these questions in the hustle and bustle of life, because we live in the world of lust and we see everything in its expansion. If we live in the world of thoughts instead of senses, then such laboratories will be able to be built, from which the seed of new thoughts, new discoveries and new philosophy can take the form of a banyan tree for the society every day!

Man can deceive himself. He may think that his knowledge grows, develops and that he has come to know and understand more than what he used to know before. But sometimes he can honestly see that before the basic riddles of existence he is as helpless as a wild man or a small child.

P. D. Ouspensky

All creations of existence are connected by a beautiful relationship

Their relationships in the entire universe are connected by an invisible thread. The texture of this relationship connects man with nature. Due to the harmonious flow of relationships, the mind of a person and the juices of the components of nature are connected with the same emotion. No one is different. It was read in the past that the green layer of moss is formed due to mutual relation between algae and fungus. Stagnant water, green and velvety moss seen on rocks and walls is an example of a kind of friendship and correlation. I wonder what the rays of the sun have to do with the greenness of a tree's leaves, a drop of water with its nourishment and an inner belief with its existence. Perhaps we also exist through such an invisible relationship, which could not be seen with any microscope till date. Food, air, and water and company of nature are the external factors of our life. But more than this, it is the invisible inner power embedded in them that keeps us alive. Connects with all the elements of nature.

There is story of my mother. She use Urdhul flowers for worship. These flowers are offered as a special offering to Mata Bhagwati. For this, mother had planted a plant of Urdhul behind the house. In the cold season, I used to prune its branch. Many flowers used to bloom on a single plant during summer. Even after plucking for worship every day, some flowers would remain on the tree. Now when the mother is no more, there are very few flowers left on the tree. The reason for this was not understood for a long time. Later its secret was understood, when I read a book. Code name God. It is written that there is a co-relation between modern science and ancient wisdom. According to the quantum field theory of physics, events in any part of the universe are related to events in other parts, that at the deepest quantum level, everything is everywhere, that is, everything is one. That is, at the level of consciousness, all the components of this universe are one - whether it is a flowering tree or my mother. Perhaps for this reason, his feelings and prayers used to affect the tree as well.

All existence has an interrelationship, which binds them together and does not allow them to separate. The world is a circle. The monolithic is dynamic. This is also because all existence is interconnected. Due to being connected with each other, there is fighting in them. The sum of our lives is juicy. Juice is flowing everywhere, which integrates man, tree, stone, animal and living and non-living being. The breath that is within us right now, the same breath goes inside another in a few moments. Where is it visible? Some first second's breath is the cause of my life in the present. Nothing is different. Similarly animals, birds, animals, trees are all inhaling and exhaling. All are one in this ocean of life. Everyone is connected. We cannot separate even by giving the names of oxygen and carbon dioxide. Trees are the reason for our life. So we and the living beings are because of their life.

Not only this, there is truth beyond this. Every day we take the juice of trees and plants in the form of food and fruits in our stomach. The same food becomes flesh, marrow, blood and brain. Then one day the body becomes dust. In this way, in the language of soil science in the form of body, nitrogen and other salts become life for trees and plants. Tree comes and goes in man and man in plant. This circle is moving. The world is moving in a continuous manner. What is in our body goes to the different elements of the universe and what is in the sun, moon, Sun, stars and trees are in plants, it comes in us. This world is family. Everything is connected here. Man is included in the stone. Man's heartbeat is linked to the moon and stars. Our thoughts are related to the waves of the ocean, the heat of the sun gives strength to our body, and then the moon causes sweetness in life. There is nothing broken here, everything is combined.

From the smallest unit of time atom today, night, seasons, celestial constellations, planets, constellations, even the universe follows the cyclic motion. Similarly, life also moves at a cyclical pace. Birth, growth, childhood, youth, adulthood, old age, death and rebirth. Circular motion. But what does one see? To man, to his speed. Not the time that sets it in motion. Because of this, everything seems to be developing linearly. While it is not the speed of time, it is the mobility of human beings. The attainment of death can be a turning point or a turning point in the dynamics of a human being for a new development. But for time it is a continuous journey. One more example to understand this. We walk on the earth, so it seems to walk linearly or in one direction or straight and slightly to and fro. But even then we are moving in circles, because this earth is round.

The resolution mantra related to socio-cultural life tells that the speed is not just circular, but conch is annular. We invoke Virat (by being small and by being small we connect ourselves with Virat. Earth is mother, Chanda is maternal uncle, sky is father, Peepal and Banyan are Baba, Ganga is mother. Not only this, the twinkling stars in the infinite distance are our relatives. There are seven sages. A pole star is the vastness of the individual. Wherein the vast universe lord dances on a spoonful of buttermilk. Whose reconnaissance is not in the control of a person, whereas Shri Ram chants a human i.e. Bharat. Indian life has bound the great in smallness and the smallness in greatness. With love and relationships, along with God, the vast and infinite planets and constellations were also added to daily life. If the mind was not satisfied with this much, then on the night of *Sharad Purnima*, *kheer* was made and kept in the open moonlight. Now since the moon is maternal uncle, he will shower his immortality and coolness on the kheer. He is immortal, so human is also immortal. This is the formula of eternity. There is a circular vision of time. For this reason, the whole movement of life is circular, that is, cyclic in the form of a conch, which was called the cycle of life. Circular means that from where we start, we reach there again after a time. Day is time for work, and night is for rest. In the same way birth is movement i.e. action and death is stop i.e. rest. Similarly creation does work and rest.

A man who is full of ambition - spiritual or worldly - can never be without problems, because problems end only when you forget the ego.

J. Krishnamurthy

It is more important to believe in life than to know

Knowing the aspects of life is the result of a long and difficult process. Because generally instead of knowing it, it is to be accepted. And it has to be understood long before that. It is like this that until we do not go through sorrow, we do not know what happiness is.

Many times such a situation comes where a person feels like questioning his decision and his discretion. When such a situation comes that all the roads seem closed. Do not see any ray of hope. Even then believe in yourself. Man makes mistakes. To believe in myself, I have realized that the most powerful weapon is prayer. Silent Prayer. In front of that God, because of whose illusion everything happens. Never lose hope of your best. Only when this happens will there be victory. It happens.

But the question is, is this life? Understand the impermanence of this life. Now making this impermanence meaningful is the main goal of life. So much time of life has passed. In search of position. Fighting Duel Got the post too. Higher and higher. Happiness also increased. Happiness too. In this, if there were some moments of trouble, then we would have become restless. Crying Shouting When the moments of happiness have passed, the moments of sorrow will also pass. Everyone will pass away.

When it was a good time, it was fine. But did we enjoy it? God does the same with us - all the time, whether before or now or later. He hurts us and we groan. But looking back, we realize that he was the one who got us out of trouble every time. We don't have to fear in life. There is always a support. Every suffering that comes in life is for the good. This leads us to a more alive and enjoyable moment.

This morning is new in the sense that it is a new year. Always used to wait for newness in life. What used to be new in childhood? Get good food or get some money in your pocket instead. Sometimes this one anna, one Chavanni used to be available, there was no limit of happiness. I used to beg my mother for this one Chavanni. He used to settle accounts with his father so that the piggy bank would be filled. Filling it was like filling the juice in life. Today I see my daughter keeps one rupee in the piggy box and she does not fill it. How can this life be full? When stomach and mind were filled in one chavni. Today even the money of the whole piggy bank or piggy box is not able to fill the stomach.

This is the age of indulgence! Don't be engrossed in action. The only goal of life. To suffer all thinking around enjoyment. Because of indulgence, we get away from ourselves. Well, the society has gone into the background. Earlier there was concern about family, society, tradition and one's heritage. There was a unified thought and behaviour. The whole world is immersed in celebration in preparation for the New Year. A dance Why is the value of one crore! Where is the society? Remembering a story of the mouse and the squirrel. There is a discussion between the two. The rat remains engrossed in the pride of being a grown up. He says I am sharp, sharp. I am a mouse whose vehicle is Lord Ganesha. That's why I am fearless. I am not afraid and I am happy. Hearing this, the squirrel said that brother, I do not have anything like this. I only believe in myself. I have a white stripe in the middle of the black stripes on my body. Means the real happiness peeps from between the layers of two difficulties. This is what I care about. Death is not visible. Only life is visible and nothing else.

In this New Year, there will be a new definition of thinking, preparation and results. Own. Of the society And to every creative person who is trying to make life meaningful. He is engaged in giving something to the society. Only indomitable creativity will assure us. Maybe even in a moment of prayer. Everything is changing in today's world. Feelings, relationships, beliefs, expectations and sensations. Their faces have changed. It is a product of time, because life itself is full of contradictions. Nothing is straight and flat so how can tomorrow be simple. Probably not. Give meaning to every moment. The success and expectation of life depends on how meaningful we are able to make the coming time in our life.

Life is infinite possibilities. That's why every day of life should be renewed. New to the mind new to the body. How is this new? Just by bringing innovation in your thoughts. Innovation sets us free. Makes you independent this is also the goal of life. There is newness every moment in the world. Our creation has been described as ever new. When newness is being born in the body every moment. But this innovation is not in our mind. The way will be found only with new songs and new moves. This newness only keeps the life of a person moving.

Is man what he seems to an astronomer? Small ball of impure carbon and water creeping like a weakling on an insignificant planet. Is there really any law of nature or are we because of our innate love for order.

Butrand Russell

Worship is the preparation to get rid of birth and death

Gentle and pious creatures take refuge in God when there is trouble and calamity in life. No pious soul wants to miss the opportunity of remembering God even in his last days. No matter what difficult times come, calamities come, they have to be welcomed. Remembrance of God is the only way to get rid of it. Mother also crossed the midstream of life by taking the help of this medium. No matter how much trouble comes in life, body becomes completely disabled, voice becomes difficult, but worship always had a place in his daily routine. It never stopped. Even on the day of his death.

Pictures of all types of deities, pirs and fakirs used to sit in his worship hall. He liked the photos of the Goddess in various postures. Wherever she goes on pilgrimage, she never forgets to buy pictures of God. Used to stand at the shop for hours and like photos. After this, she used to decorate it with great devotion in the worship house. The worship house is small, he would have regretted it. I used to say that the house of worship is not small, the list of your gods is so big that the house of worship becomes small. But these things have no effect on him. I used to say many times - Mother, there is only one God. Whether you worship Ram or Durga ji. It doesn't make any difference. She would say - we all know. Lekin tohra bujhat naikhe nu. Don't look at Sarasatiji for the sake of knowledge. Ramji did not give money. God is one and He has various powers. I realized this only through him. Maa Durgaji's special aarti during Navratri - Jagjanani Jai Jai. It was only during this bhajan that these voices of praise used to come – You are Ram, Krishna, you are Vrajrani Radha.... It was only after this bhajan that in my youth I realized the multidimensional power of the One God.

Learned instinctively from mother that the meaning of worship is praise, hymns and rituals. In the second phase it comes the time for chanting, silent meditation. She used to see both hymns and praises linked to the worship of God. Although this is also a type of prayer. But there is a difference between the two. Bhajan means hymn. Means worshiping God and attaining Him. The word bhajan is used for religious songs. Kirtan is composed of narration. Any narration in relation to God with different rhythms, ragas and taals and rhymes is called Pratibha Bhajan. The hymns of Sur, Tulsi and Meera are world famous. But praise is a part of the worship system. It means song of praise and praise. In short, praising God is praise. It is a form of prayer, in which a person connects with God and desires to get something from him. Fear and selfishness act as a catalyst in this. Most of the people pray only because some of their wishes are fulfilled. Spirituality is different from prayer, hymn or praise. In this a person merges himself in the divine power of any expectation or fear.

Mai was also full of spirituality. The biggest reason for this was not due to his prayer or divine company. There were two main reasons for this. First of all she was illiterate. Didn't have alphabet knowledge at all. This is the reason that all his hymns or praises or prayers in Shruti. Shrinkage is the nature of the small mind, whose heart is firm and whose conduct is confirmed by conscience, they bear their principles till death comes.

Even if we sit and watch the empty sky for a while, the emptiness of the sky will make us empty. Will start to lighten and clean the garbage and heaviness of our inner self. If we sit near a flower, we will forget everything in a while, and the smell of flowers will make us fragrant. Similarly, if we see the sun with our eyes, then the energy of the sun will be illuminated in the form of light inside us. Be it the waves of the ocean or the murmur of the river. There will be a feeling in their proximity that we too are flowing like an ocean. It is just necessary to find something to pause in life. It is necessary to know life. Was teaching my daughter only yesterday. It was on my mind to read it the full text today. Suddenly she got up while reading. I asked what happened. Study is over, now it's break. Why, I asked? She says that even in school one gets some time after a period. Need a break to think. For remembering. Suddenly my mind flashed-daughter is right. Be it studies or job or any other work. A break is necessary at some intervals. At least for freshness, new thought and enthusiasm.

For rest, man first discovered a cave, then built a hut and then built a house. Even a bird flying in the infinite sky has to make a small nest. It is necessary to fly the nest. To fly, you have to combine power. In this journey of life, we can make use of the world, do not run away from it. For this rest is necessary. You should always do your own assessment. As human beings we have become very busy. Those delicate activities of our life have reduced or ended, which make our life beautiful. Communicates peace, happiness and joy in life. The fabric of the modern world is missing the pause button, which used to be involuntarily pressed at the sight of beautiful flowers, twinkling stars, the first shower of monsoon, a friend or relative visiting home. If there is no time left in our life for great creations, melodious music, charming pictures, fragrant relations, interesting nature, then it has to be accepted that the flow of modern life suppresses us.

The person who stands by the truth makes steady progress with the values. When his values increase him fame and prestige, he becomes an infallible source of power and greatness.

Maharishi Dayanand Saraswati

Search for life partner

When we are happy, everything looks good. And it gets better. But when the time is not right, even good looks bad. We all want to move forward, but do not want to accept the risk associated with it. The problem of a human being is that he always seeks or wants such a partner, who is compatible with his mind. Happy, okay. If there is sorrow, sadness, then it is bad. If someone's advice is useful, then it is okay. Otherwise the human race itself is wrong. If I try to put it in another form, if the mind is positive, then everything is fine, otherwise it is negative, then we do not believe in ourselves what is right and what is wrong. Don't trust yourself. Human beings do not like the life of sadness and sorrow but they are also not under their control. Yes! It is true that even a little happy moment comes in life, then the wings get attached. We start flying. There is such a communication of courage, where the confidence to do anything is generated.

Positivity is not a thing, not an intellectual thing. This is the state of the individual. Finding a new path in life, feeling the fragrance of a flower, making the day innovative and the night memorable. All this is possible when there is something in the person. How do these situations arise? Sometimes I think of something good, I can write well. I do some good work. But sometimes nothing good can happen even after wishing. After thinking closely, it was found that it is due to making life monotonous. No partner in life. Companion means catalyst. Many times in childhood I used to think that what is the catalyst for me? Where does the inspiration for goodness come from? I used to search for this since childhood. Liked some things, he would have adopted them. Later it came to know that inspiration can be taken from all these things, situations and things. Remember, when I was young, my mother used to take me for worship by holding my hand. Peepal trees, Banyan and Tulsi trees on the day of Vat Savitri, Banana trees on Thursdays, Amla trees in the month of Kartik. worship and contemplation sitting under them. There was a sequence of worship. Kul Devi, Gram Devi, Kul Devta, Brahm Sthan, Saton Bahini, followed by the prestigious temples of the region etc. These things taught us that a person is small in front of the vastness of the universe, but there is a sequence, the last step of which makes a man the best man. There is an opportunity to interpret specific definitions of life with nature. Nature means what? Water, forest, soil, mountain, wind, tree, sky. When these five elements of nature reside in our body, if we want to move forward in the world, then how will we be able to move forward without the blessings of nature?

I remember my childhood. If something new had to be done, father would have taken all of us brothers and sisters to the fair in a bullock cart. Many times I would go to the market sitting on a bicycle. Remember climbing mango trees in summer, bathing in the pond, playing marbles, gilli-danda, pitto, hide and seek, thief-soldier. Buying vegetables himself for the first time and saving four annas, eight annas out of it. Mother's fasting every month and on the pretext of making sweets and cooking something different from the routine at home. People would come and go, and the discussion would go on endlessly. Sometimes the discussion was meaningful, and sometimes just like that. All of these have important contributions. In the development of our social spirit, in deepening the family relation and in keeping that thread alive forever. Sports, worship, and travel remind us of the smell of the earth, the scent of nature, the music of life, and the interdependence between them all.

Who are the companions in life? Only humans or animals or birds or anything else. If there is travel, there is development, then the companion cannot be only a person, animal or any creature. Having a partner depends on the relation or relationship. Sometimes a person or even his family does not seem like a companion, and sometimes everything from trees and plants to ponds, rivers, mountains, forests, ant to forest creatures and these planets and constellations all seem to be ours. After all, something will happen that in faraway California J, Krishnamurti becomes one with the rag trees, in the secluded place of Pondicherry, in the middle of the sea, some Maharishi Aurobindo and Swami Vivekananda find their companions, who show them the truth. Similarly, sometimes a memorable moment, a heart touching song, a memorable book, moments spent with nature can also be companions. Companion means give reminder, give source of light, and show the path of goodness. And then a flower, a drop of rain, the twinkling of lamps at a distant temple in the dark night, a sweet sound, a picture can turn our despair into hope. Can make a believer. Remembering, poet Rabindranath

Tagore's world famous poem- *Ekla Chalo Re*. And the tone of a film song made on this sentiment-
Walk alone walk alone,.
Your fair is left behind, walk alone.
Would have called you here to bear the sorrows.
There is no human being who has not suffered.

In the present life, when in the era of cleverness and bhagambhag, (Every time Racing) it seems strange to see the changing form of the partner. I miss my mother, I feel like remembering Baba (My grandfather), who gave the sense of Vasudhaiva Kutumbakam through Karma and Dharma during his lifetime?

Man's purposes and goals are to be found within a vast circular universe. Which has no goal of its own. Nature is a game, it has no purpose of its own. And the possibility that he has no purpose in the future and the possibility that he has no goal in the future. He doesn't have any flaws.

Alan watts

No development of consciousness means waiting for death.

There is a Russian story - Life. Many chickens were fighting with each other in a big basket. The lower one flaps to come up after dropping the upper one to breathe in the open air. Everyone is troubled by hunger and thirst. Meanwhile, the butcher comes with a knife. Holding each and every chicken by the neck, pulling it out of the basket, cutting it back and throwing it away. A torrent of hot blood bursts from the body of a slaughtered chicken. The other live chickens inside pounce on it to extinguish the fire in their belly. In the snatching of their living beaks, the head of a dead chicken bounces and rolls like a ball. The butcher continues to cut the chicken in the crate. The number of sharers also decreases within the basket. In this happiness, bang is also heard once in a while among the rest of the cocks. In the end the crate is filled with all the slaughtered chickens. There is silence all around, there is no quarrel or noise.

Such is life. Everyone is waiting for death here. Every moment someone's neck is cut, but those whose neck is not cut, they are in competition. This is the stage of dialectical development of life. Birth-death, happiness-sorrow, loss-gain. The truth is that there is neither happiness nor sorrow in life. There is neither life nor death. Overall, this is logic. This is the satisfaction of the mind. Man does not want anyone's company in life. But the difficulty is that everyone keeps coming together and gradually leaves. Who wants someone to meet and leave! There is a film song - *Duniya Yeh Duniya Toofan Mail*. Its wheels would go loud and go on their way. Children consider it a game. Someone would have booked a ticket somewhere. One comes, one goes. The mail is of a moment. The one who keeps as much capital as he has, travels that much. Tells the difference of life. The wise say Rail. This world is really a mail storm. Where does the world remember those who were left out? Where is the leisure? Many leave at the stations of this life and many come. But.... As easy as it is to say, difficult to understand. The common man remembers the philosophy in the crematorium or in solitude. But where does life go with philosophy. There are established beliefs and traditions for that. There is a system.

That's why it is necessary that we do not run away from the world while living in the world. Rather, do continuous development of consciousness in life. Not only of physical life, but also of inner life. Because the relaxation that is being sought. It started when the man came out of the cave. After that he built a hut and then built a house. Now grand house is being built, but there is no peace anywhere. Now it is being talked about that peace is not in the outer limit but in the infinite. This is the last nest of life. Then there is no need to build more houses across it. If you get shelter in the eternal and eternal home, then why stay in the temporary and perishable home. One has to know oneself to rest in the infinite. Everyone in the world can become a king but we want to live as beggars. All are slaves. Know how to ask Sometimes from God, sometimes from manager, sometimes from self. As long as we keep on traveling in the outside world, there is no way for our prosperity.

Making king in the earthly world, it is impossible to win. Will get defeated one day. There is only one world, the world of the self. Where a man can be king. And by becoming the king of the inner kingdom, a person can remain a king outside as well. But there is so much jealousy, malice, greed and lust in the outside kingdom that no one can become a king. The story is that there was a King of Prussia in German. Fredrik the Great. One evening while taking a walk, he bumped into an old man. Expressing displeasure, Fredrik asked who you are. Don't know me that old man replied that I am the king. Fredik was surprised but then he asked which country do you rule? That old man said that on himself.

Let's see the spread of the tree. Feel the smell of its flowers and fruits. The dance of the leaves is visible in the rays of the sun, but where the life of the tree is, we cannot see it. Similarly where the root of life is. We do not see, because the journey of our consciousness is external. Nothing will be gained in this external journey. Only death will happen! The fullness of life lies in the inner journey. There is the abode of God. Life is within, expansion is outside. When the mind does not act, the doors of consciousness open. Then the eye sees the world even in a small flower. The whole world is hidden in each leaf. The whole vast leela in a single molecule. The journey of life is the journey of discovering this great Leela.

The one who surrounds us from all sides. To us who is also within us. And it is in our breath. Without which we cannot be and we were not, even then what was. And we will not be, even then what will remain. That sky is the element.

HP Balavatsky

Body as an object

No matter how much you keep searching through the senses, only matter comes into contact with the senses. It has limits, like the eye. You can see with your eyes, but you cannot hear. You can hear its type with your ears, but you cannot see it. The hand has the limitation that it can touch but cannot smell. For this the nose is necessary. But one sense can do only one thing, the other cannot. Nothing in life can happen to the soul. Whatever happens is happening on the body. Whatever it touches, it touches the body. This house is collapsing. But there is a misconception that I am the body.

The Supreme Soul resides in this temple like body. We have been searching since eternity but do not find it. What is within, is sought outside. It is basically a fault. Our body is not opposite to the divine. This is the temple, this is the place of worship. This is the place of God. Osho says that we have been told that the body is sin. When we accept the sin of the body, when we make a house of lust, we will never find God. For this reason we are afraid to do the inner journey of the body. Meditation is the medium of the inner journey of the body. Who teaches us the art of sitting inside? We have to connect ourselves with the divine i.e. light. There God is always waiting for us. He always makes a sound, calls out. The beat is his voice. He stands, he waits but we don't go to meet him. Our journey is external, it is of lust. There are many stages in the journey. The first stop is the body. The second stage is the heart. This is the journey of the gross. Then there is silence, concentration and meditation in the journey of consciousness.

Zen story. Bokuju was a master. He lived in a cave. All alone But when he was alone, he would say - Bokuju. This was his name. Then he himself would answer. Sir, I am here. Then there was no one to be his disciple. He would say that whenever I start drowning in thought, I have to wake myself up. And that's why I call my name. At that very moment the thoughts go away. In the last days of life, the disciples said that now you do not call your name. Then the Guru said that there is no need for it. Now Bokuju is always present. Whenever you are in deep worry, call your name. The body of every human being is "his" temple. There is no purity in our eyes. There is no prayer in the breaths. He does not have good thoughts in his mind. When these things are not in our personality then stay outside the temple or enter inside. How does it matter? Going to God and asking for something less than God is the identity of our pettiness and it is an insult in a way. It also means that what we ask has become more important than God.

In this world a body becomes a Buddha. In this world there is a body called Krishna. And one body becomes Jesus. And in this world we cannot become anything. The world from which all things are drawn. It is exactly one - the one sky, the same fire pervading all, the one wind blowing all around. That land is also the only one which stabilizes us. He is all one, but we become different. Our bodies are one. There are many similarities in our body structure. Same blood, same bone, flesh and marrow. But the personality of the man becomes different. Some man becomes Buddha. Some stand in the dark and some cannot find their way even in the light.

The body which we see as a solid physical structure is also like an object. To whom diseases bind. Old age has to be faced and eventually it has to end. This body is not our real form. There is no significant difference between human and animal at the level of the body. All the basic functions of the body – pleasure, pain, eating and drinking, birth and death, sleep and indolence, breathing and reproduction are common in us and in animals. There is no difference. The story is that when Adam and Eve saw themselves naked for the first time, they were scared. But he rejected his animal nature, which resulted in Form he could distinguish between his existence and body. In the world of religion and spirituality, the difference between the body and the self was understood. But despite this, this body has as much complexity as this whole universe. There is no shortage of complexity in it. And in one sense, we are more complex than the universe. Because the expansion of the body is less but the complexity is like the universe. There are seven crore bacteria in one body. There is a big colony of seven crore cells. There are some three billion nerve fibres in a tiny brain. If the whole city is not in order, we will not be able to enter inside. It requires silence, rhythmicity, peace and cheerfulness.

Once a devotee asked Raman Maharshi - Who am I? Maharishi said that I am not the gross body made of seven metals. I am not even the five sense organs that perceive the subjects like sound, touch, form, smell, smell. I am not even the five senses of speech, movement, eclipse, excreta and enjoyment. I am not even the Panchakarma Vayu who does breathing and exhalation etc. I am not even the mind that makes a resolution. I am not even ignorance with sensual desires. Then the disciple asked Guru, so who am I? Then Raman Maharshi said that after all this only Chaitanya remains, which you is. And his form is Sachchidananda (The Truth, the goodness and the happiness). And the body becomes important only after the visit of this form. Only then our body will be able to become a means to enter the state of inner peace.

Those who will really call out to God with a true heart. Their cry will definitely be heard and they will definitely get what they have asked for and desired.

Martin Luther
Bring the tree to the centre of life for inner happiness

Know the nature before understanding the relationship between nature and life. What is nature? In fact, this creation originated from nature itself. Nature which consists of the basic five elements. Earth, water, air, fire and sky. These five elements are the basic elements and this is also the basis of the life of human beings and other living beings. Since the creation of nature in the form of creation is also basically done from these five elements. Therefore nature and human i.e. life cannot be separated from each other. This is the umbilical cord connection. Without nature, life would be destroyed. Human existence will end.

Our life is dependent on nature. Whereas we understand that nature is the object of our enjoyment. It is not an enjoyment but a matter of coincidence. Coincidence means to preserve and use. Life is dependent on nature because it receives nourishment from nature. Nature itself provides him food and air and water, only then life is sustained. Otherwise life will never be saved. Nowadays, the meaning of nature is applied only to the earth, which is not correct. The range of nature extends to the gross universe, in which the sun, moon and stars and planets and satellites also come. When nature is discussed, environment also comes in it and the life of humans and other living beings. No one is different anywhere.

Environmental awareness is embedded in our human consciousness. Nature has always been respected in the Indian thought tradition. From mountains, rivers, sun, moon to trees and plants, reverence has been a part of our daily life. In this contemplative tradition, God is not somewhere in a temple or a temple, but he has been in front of us in the forms of various elements of nature, such as: earth, water, fire, air and sky. Not only had this, in Indian spirituality it has been defined as Tatvbodh i.e. the basic concepts of nature. When we go away from nature, then only we pollute it. Now the time has come to revive once again those traditions of the past, in which so much reverence was requested for nature. It is often argued that there is bound to be a threat to nature due to technological development. But this is not necessary. Sustainable development can be achieved only when nature is preserved and protected. Science and technology should never be considered as anti-nature components. On the contrary, we should think about how to preserve the environment along with the development of science and technology. This is the biggest challenge today.

Pay attention to nature. All the five elements of nature are different from each other. The job of water is to extinguish the fire. Fires and flares up in the presence of air. Similarly, countless living beings live with nature.

Birds, mammals, reptiles. All of them have enmity towards others in their nature. Despite this, nature keeps a balance between all. It never happens that nature has destroyed a species just like that.

In the same way, there is no pollution in spite of having so many living beings in the forest and nature. We need to learn a lot from nature. How nature assimilates the garbage and re-creates something beautiful from it. Similarly, there is no danger from science and technology, but as a result of technological and scientific process, waste is created.

A tree is important in our life. And even if everything is forgotten, it has to be remembered with every breath that with every falling tree, our breath of life is also decreasing. The way the earth is proving to be a dwarf in the indiscriminate race of civilization. Civilization is on the verge of war over water. The day is not far when people will yearn for pure oxygen. It is not necessary that the state-of-the-art technology is always economically useful and favourable. We should draw conclusions on the basis of merits and demerits of the technique.

Our body is constantly affected by the external environment. Earth's atmosphere affects our body Apart from this, the planets, satellites and constellations outside the earth also affect our body completely, because the whole universe is connected in one thread. If an event happens in space, then its effect is felt on the earth. And all the creatures of the earth are affected by it. Franz Mesmer has written a book - The Influence of the Planet on Human Body. In this book he has written that whatever happens in the universe, every living being in the universe gets affected by it. If this was not the case, then even today people would not be afraid of the seven and a half years of the planet Saturn located far away.

Earth is our own home and we are members of one family. It is natural that all the incidents happening on earth will have an effect on our body. When winter comes, the coldness of the earth affects our body and in the same way heat and rain affect our body. God has filled the entire nature with greenery. Trees, plants, bushes, forests, flowering plants etc. are all green in colour. Green color is beneficial for our body and health. There is a principle of science that if there is coldness in the outside environment then that coldness enters inside through the pores of our skin. As soon as the cold enters inside, then a green liquid starts coming out from the body, which in the language of science is called TRPM-III. Perhaps that's why the creators of the universe made green trees, bushes, grass, green vegetables and small plants adjacent to the ground on the earth so that these green leaves can absorb more heat from the sun and give us relief.

The meaning of knowledge is not only to know something through the intellect, but to make it a part of one's existence by experiencing it with the whole heart and soul. If a person practices untruth, even if he proclaims the supremacy of truth, he cannot have true faith in the supremacy of truth.

Socrates

The search for the light of knowledge and character

Om Saha Navavatu. With nine roasters. Cum semen is done.

Tejaswi Navadhitamastu. I am a scholar. Om. Peace: Peace: Peace.

Kathopanishad

O God! You protect both of us (guru and disciple) in every way. May you nurture both of us (teacher and disciple) together properly, may you simultaneously strengthen us both (as a result of study) in every way. Lest we be defeated by anyone in education and be bound by the thread of mutual affection throughout life. There should never be any feeling of hatred between us. O God! May we retire from all three heat?

This peace lesson is described in many Upanishads. This peace text is a wonderful and enduring gesture of the Indian Upanishads, which has been giving inspiration and light to Indian civilization and knowledge for thousands of years. Education is the joint pursuit of knowledge and elevation of character by teacher and disciple. It is a co-operative enterprise. The teacher gives and the disciple takes. For this reason both also exchange inspiration and light. All learning begins and ends with wonder, but the first wonder is the child of ignorance and the second wonder the father of worship. The meaning of education is not to stuff the brain but to enlighten the mind and heart. The first goal of education is *Tejaswi Navadhitamastu.* The one who was in darkness should become enlightened. For this purpose man acquires knowledge. This is followed by the second ultimate goal – *Ma Vidvishav Hai.* That is, we should not hate each other.

Neil Ferguson, a British historian wrote a book - Civilization. In this he has tried to prove that western civilization means Britain. Also, even though different civilizations of the world consider themselves great. You have been great but today the life of the whole world is going on according to or shown by the western civilization. Spoon-knife and fork in food, brush in mouth, shoe and stocking on feet, pant, coat and tie on body are being used today by the whole world. Everyone uses the chair and table. There should be commode in the toilets of the house, modular kitchen in the kitchen. He has influence everywhere. From colloquialism, lifestyle to political system is also the gift of Britain. Democracy, which is the best system of governance, was also developed by Britain to rule North America.

India was far ahead of the whole world till the 18th century, but after that the situation in the world changed. Why did this happen? *Kathopanishad* gives the answer to this. We emphasized on the love side of Vidya, which was pleasant for us. We rejected the credit, which was good for the society. Lack of inquisitive mind, there was a famine at the level of contemplation and thoughts. The day the inquisitive Guru stopped taking birth in India, our downfall started on the same day. Texts like Upanishads could not be written even after thousands of years. Today, every home and family has to be made a laboratory, that is, an incubator. The parents themselves will have to become its teachers. We have to tell that those who study from Arts subject are not only going to get the benefit of physical degree but its real human value is also embedded in it. Similarly, the study of science should aim at uncovering the secrets of nature.

In the dialogue between Yamraj and Nachiketa, Yama taught Nachiketa like a teacher. In Kathopanishad they say that neither Twa Kama Bahvodlolupant. That is, many enjoyments and luxuries did not distract you. The lofty idea of education is where excellence of knowledge and character is sought. In the Upanishads, if education cannot rise above the subjective life, then it loses its quality. Sits and becomes ignorance. Vidya is that which frees the human soul from the slavery of the subjects – *sa vidya ya vimuktaye*. Education is not just an education to earn bread or prepare for the benefits of the world. If education does not lead to all-round development, then that life remains a narrow life.

There has been a tradition of Rishi and Guru i.e. Acharya in Indian life. It is the Rishi tradition that has been doing the regulation of the system. Sages like Vishwamitra, Krishna, Chanakya, Vidyaranya, Ramdas and Vivekananda always worked to awaken, organize and organize the nation. Parallel to this there was also an Acharya tradition i.e. Guru Tradition, which continued from Vashisht, Sandipani to Narayan Guru, Jyotiba Phule in modern times. The Guru is a companion in the new search for knowledge with his disciple. But now that tradition of Guru has ended. The reason for India's character, moral and spiritual decline is the disappearance of ideals and values in education along with its creditable goal. Education is actually a life-long process, in which the art of thinking, creating and development is learned. But where is any guru today? Which is always present in front of our consciousness in the form of truth.

To touch a stone is to touch a piece of the eternal. Praying in a way that at least the love of this evening, the longing of this dark hour, will not pass away, will survive among these ruins for years to come.

Nirmal Verma

The search for Shriram lies in the ascension of consciousness

Shriram is pervaded in every particle of India, in every person and in every mind. His name echoes from huts to attics. Shriram is the name of the one element that connects every part of India, mountains, oceans, forests, plains. Seven thousand years ago Shri Ram had united the whole country, so even today the country can be united in his name. Shri Ram is present in the consciousness of every Indian. Because the purest model of consciousness is Rama. Remembering Shri Ram is not enough. We have to find them within ourselves first. In the journey of a person's life, if Shri Ram is not included in our heart, then his remembrance is useless. Who is Ram? He is not a man, he is Purushottam. They are credit. His life journey is the ascension of the male towards Narayan.

In Indian society, Lord Shiva, Shri Krishna, Mahavir, Durga and other Gods dominate the public mind. But more than this, when it comes to building a person, Ram is more favorable. They are closer to our consciousness. Keeping the photo of Ram Darbar in the house symbolizes that everything is in perfect condition in the family. This is the reason that the name of Ram is the truth from birth till death. The Brihadaranyaka Upanishad states that you are what your deepest desire is. As is your wish, there is your aspiration. As is your desire, so is your action, as is your action, so is your destiny. Today everyone wants development, aspires to become the best. But there is adjustment in the will and deeds of some people. The greatest potential for growth is in times of change. We want development but not change. The period of change is often sad. The person who understands the power of change, will become the

Carrier of that change. Shri Ram had understood him. Shri Ram had understood the pathetic condition of present day India. India binds the country in one thread - from north to south. He did not make the dynasty or royal place synonymous with materiality as the development center of civilization, but made the archetypes of powerless, sources of power - forest, nature.

If 14 years of Rama's life in exile and a few months with Vishwamitra are removed, then nothing will be left. And in this the story of struggle and his becoming Purushottam is included. Whatever you want to achieve in life, you have to become it. For that development of consciousness is necessary. The situation was clear in Shriram's mind and the goals were also clear. Just like that, he did not set out in the north direction with Vishwamatri. Even before this, at the age of 15, he had made a pilgrimage to the whole of India. After the journey, disinterest arose in him, so the father sent him to Guru Vasishtha. The detailed description of the dialogue between Guru and Shriram is in Yogavasistha. When he went to take permission from Mata Kaushalya for exile, he said - where all kinds of peacocks are available. That means now a big task has to be done. He was already preparing for this. Consciousness is the center of all physical, mental and spiritual power. The development of consciousness was always the only goal of Shri Ram. He knew that if you want to bring yourself to the state of Purushottam, then only work, devotion, struggle and best feelings can be ideal. He always had faith in himself, even when father Dasaratha had doubts about fighting the demon, wife Sita about breaking the bow and Vibhishana about killing Ravana.

He was always working for the continuous ascent of consciousness. He constantly tried to imbue his consciousness with the lofty feelings of life, to accept that which is better for the society than the beloved, to devote the mind to a noble goal beyond duality, to have a character free from attachment and hatred. be constructed There is also emotion and sensitivity in Ram's life. When Bharata comes to meet Ramji in the forest, Shri Ram meets his brother with emotion, but immediately rejects it firmly when it comes to Rajpat. There is an old tradition of knowing this society through traveling and pilgrimage of India. Sri Krishna, Buddha, Chanakya, Shankaracharya, Vivekananda and Mahatma Gandhi are prominent names in this century. All of them ascended their consciousness on this earth. The skyline of Indian history when great men Mahatma Gandhi came on the horizon of Indian politics, and became a Mahatma by his deeds, thoughts and life. Such a Mahatma who did not do japa-penance, did not go to temple, did not grow hair and did not make ashrams and disciples.

Shri Ram never considered himself as the doer. Took birth from the womb of mother Kaushalya. Lived a human life in childhood, no charisma like Shri Krishna. His life proceeds in a smooth and simple manner.

Always keep ideals in front of yourself. Ideal i.e. after setting the goal, work is done on a double level. Choose the option of struggle at the external level. At the inner level, the work of the ascension of consciousness is done. At the outer level Maharishi obeys every order of Vishwamatri, goes to exile for the society. Remember - Dasharatha's order was not - to go to exile. But knowing the meaning hidden in Kaikeyi's boon, Shriram took the path of exile and saved his father from dishonor. During father's death, separation from wife, conversation with brother, control your impulses, emotions and excitement. The expression of thoughts is based on the choice of words. He always understood the power of words. He was well aware of the consequences and power of his disclosure. While talking with Nishadraj, Kevat, Shabari, he shows softness, whereas in the struggle with Tadka, Maricha, Bali, Ravana, he shows the hardness. Be it conversation with Maharishi Parshuram or dialogue with Jatayu or use of words with Hanuman. The level of their expressions and tone is different in every place.

Purity of soul is a journey of a different path. How to conduct life between the demands of the body and the influence of nature? This was shown by Shri Ram. Since childhood. Living among brothers encourage them. Salvation of Ahilya, conversation with Parshuram, seeing Sita for the first time, observing decorum during the meal in marriage, following the vow of monogamy after marriage. After all, how did Shri Ram become the pinnacle of dignity? This is a subject of research! This dignity which is the demand of present India. The call of the society remains. There has become a need for a balance between market and enjoyment. Shri Ram is remembered. Why ? India's identity, its spiritual heritage is now trapped in the maze of fear and indulgence. If it is to be saved, then Ram is the only solution.

God is everywhere. It is in matter, it is in water, it is in air and sky. He is beyond all these. We call it Brahma. So sometimes God. Actually this is the power which decides the creation, condition and rhythm of the world.

Ramanujacharya

Self-discovery in the rut away from life

This age is of enjoyment, of sense pleasures. And to see myself on top. A dark journey we think that we have gone too far. We feel that we are also moving forward but no. The roots of life and the juice contained in it were left behind, or dried up, which survived till a few years after independence. In this new age, a person is growing rapidly with time. Where are you going? what is the direction Nothing is known. Everyone is just busy flowing. Hindi Writer; Nirmal Verma writes in his novel *Antim Aranya* that - look back a little, just like we look back a little and look at a painting. We will feel how wrong we are. We try to listen, we try to see. Don't just go on walking but we are going on walking.

This is a vicious circle or a delusion in which fulfilment of one's desire, for this duality, running around and being engrossed in one's own world is becoming the goal of life. Many things that go away from life are just left in the memory. Breaking the morsels while sitting in the pangat (in line collectively). The insistence of mother, aunt and grandmother to take more has become a thing of the past. Now in the era of buffet, all the food items will be found decorated on the table. Used to eat while sitting, so used to eat less. If you eat while standing, more food goes into the stomach. Along with this, diseases also come. Today I remember that where those lines, which used to connect relationships are. The village barber used to give orders in every house for invitation to eat and the message of victory when the food was ready. Where is that grandma? When he used to go round the village with his stick. The chain of fables, proverbs, stories and proverbs used to start while sleeping. Even today there is Dadi and Nani and the story. But TV came in place of grandmother and serial took the place of the story. Now when the eyes open after sleeping, there is a hurry to take the children to school. We are at the crossroads in the blink of an eye. Then the first sleep used to open, then the voice of mother's Aarti used to fall in the ear. Home used to be the first school. Now A, B, C...'s Shree Ganesh gets the school done. We make him practice at home. Then there was the lesson of culture and culture, in spite of that one can laugh out loud. Today, laughing openly is a sign of rudeness. If you are happier, then you can smile.

Man is going away from himself. There is a man, there is a house. AC to avoid heat in the house. There is an oven to cook food, a washing machine to clean clothes, and a heater in winter. But we have also started keeping a thermometer to measure relationships moment by moment. I remember, we were not rich then. There were less clothes in the house. But there was no shortage. In winter, mother used to chill herself, but she used to keep us brothers covered. Used to wear half pants till matriculation, father had bought a full pant to take the exam and got the opportunity to tie a watch on his hand after passing. Today, even after having clothes, we became naked. Shameless in fashion. Earlier, I used to jump in the field barefoot, I used to like it. Muddy feet, wet body in the rain, mother's scolding and oil massage used to give a feeling of being together forever in our life. Today I am afraid to set foot in the field, because the shoes worn on the feet come to mind. The fear of getting soiled haunts me. If you are afraid of soil, then it is natural to be away from reality. Whole grains reduce belly fat. No one told us this. It was part of life. Used to eat bread made of coarse flour, thekua.

Corn cobs used to be a rainy evening snack. Raw gram, reed, guava, carrot, papaya were part of the routine. The body did not need daily exercise. When he used to cycle for 10 to 15 kms, that itself was a part of exercise. Where did we know that there is physical exercise in the gym?

There are 1000 channels on TV at home, when you step out of the house, there are dozens of malls and multiplexes. After this we have mobile for 24 hours. There is Facebook, WhatsApp, Twitter etc. on mobile, which every moment gives the message of information by ticking. Where are we with ourselves? It has taken away the topic of our dialogue, our conversation. Simple and easy relationships of our life have been made commercial. Now our sociality is limited to likes, comments and ok. It is not a very old thing. When everyone knew in whose house the dish was being prepared, in whose house the guest came and in whose house the parrot escaped by breaking the cage. In whose house the daughter is married and in whose house who is sick. When a thief broke into someone's house, all the doors of the village were opened. It was a social concern, which used to be the strength of the village and locality. When the dish was made, it was offered to Kuldevi to Gramdevi, distributed in the neighbourhood, then the people of the house would take it in the form of Prasad. Today that oily dish has become a part of our daily life. Earlier, when a daughter got married in the village, the whole village used to gather. If any unknown person had entered the village, there would have been so many questions as if that person was appearing for a competitive exam. Such concern had its own meaning. Today many flats in one apartment. Walls are one, ladder is one, and lift is also one. Even after this, there is no time to talk to people standing side by side and there is no need to even look away. Who is there, where to go? Asking this is a sign of rudeness. We keep such thoughts ourselves, and create them in our children as well. Such thinking has dug the grave of our social concern.

We didn't even know when crime and terror started prevailing around us because of being confined to ourselves! Today, in place of family, nuclear family, home instead of house and harmony and interdependent society, opportunistic selfish society is taking place. Is. Now our world is shrinking only till our family, our home. A world where there is a big 30 inch TV, plenty of food, luxury and everyone is confined to themselves, busy. No one has time for anyone. Where are we worried about our childhood? When a child is not taught about culture, tradition and ideals, then from where will he think about the nation? Think, when do we get to spend time for ourselves? In this case, where will the creation come from? From where will the search for the self-take place? When you do not know yourself, then every attempt to know the world will be unsuccessful.

The multiplicity of Brahman is like the moon whose many forms appear in pots, rivers and ponds filled with water. Similarly, one Brahman is present in many living beings. He neither creates any kind of creation nor annihilation. This is Maya which is the manifestation of the subjects of the world.

Adi Shankaracharya

Where do we bow our heads in life?

We know that money is waste. There is no limit to enjoyment. Where does position and prestige always remain? Rushing, running and worrying in life is useless. Even after this nothing is left. There is always a desire for something else. Due to the desire for something else and the fear of tomorrow, a person visits temples, deities, mountains, forests, pilgrimages, rivers, tombs and various places of worship throughout his life. Bows his head. Prays. Along with this, he asks for something for himself or his near and dear ones from Baba, saints and sadhaks in different forms of God or divine power. A web of dreams is woven and every possible effort is made to achieve it.

Man either worships or worships God because of fear. Or there is a desire to get something in his mind. In the early days of civilization, we used to bow our heads before Indra, Varuna, Agni, river, tree and mountain. Later on, Brahma, Vishnu and Mahesh bowed down with it considering them as deities. Earlier they used to worship in the open sky, in the cave of the mountains and under the tree. Later, he built temples, chaityas, mathas, invented prayers in the form of mantras and hymns, so that he could offer his devotion to God.

The question is whether a man should go on pilgrimage, bathe at the confluence of holy rivers or go to the shelter of any awakened deity. What will it take? Perform Yajna rituals, sing praises, do bhajans and kirtans. After this, put your greed in front of God. Request your wish, sorrow. It is a deal that we prayed, now you give the prasad. This is the reason why sorrow does not end even after taking refuge in these divinity, worries do not go away. In such a situation, there is a need to look inside yourself. Mahatma Buddha in his Dhammapada through a beautiful formula has given the mantra of this condition of a person and how to get out of it. They say that- man should bow before the tree, or should he bow before the mountain, or should he bow before the river. What will it take? Anything can happen only if humans bow down to wisdom.

We cannot be liberated by going to the shelter of that which gives rise to sorrow and misery. We bow down throughout our lives, but never before an awakened person or before a tree or idol full of compassion. Do not bow down before. Also, when we bow down, do not bring desire and lust in between. There are many such people in this world, whom we generally reject even after recognizing them. An awakened and spiritual man is not necessarily a Mahatma. He could be a daily wage labourer, a farmer working in the field, a village woman selling vegetables. When we cannot bow down to the understanding of the awakened soul, then prayer and effort to find the deity in any stone or soil are mere illusions. It is a means to satisfy your ego and a means to satisfy fear and greed.

Today, Baba, we are standing in the market place of sages and saints, where we kneel down due to fear, indulgence and greed. By going to these shelters, there is no relief from sorrows, sorrows only increase. The refuge of Babas and Gods is not the right refuge. Similarly, if one does not give up greed and selfishness, then what if it rains a hundred gold, even then the person's hunger will not end. Mahatma Buddha says look at me. I come home where it's raining gold, but even that can't stop me. The fulfilment of any desire is short-lived. In the end it will only hurt.

Knowing the truth, only if you bow down, it will be auspicious refuge. Mahatma Buddha says in his Dhammapada that even if there is rain of gold, man's works are not satisfied. All material pleasures are tasteless and painful. That's why we have to agree in our little happiness and sorrow. He was constantly engrossed in the search for truth. From one guru to another. Wherever you got knowledge, bow your head there. Alar Kalam was his teacher, after attaining knowledge, he was expressed his desire to stay in Gurukul and to be given Gurupad. Mahatma Buddha rejected. He said where to stop till the interview of the truth? Where did Nachiketa stay? If money, position and prestige were needed, then all the happiness of the world was at his feet. He never showed his head attachment towards worldly things.

Today is a strange time. Everywhere our head bows, from where we get something. In such a situation, character building is the most important task. Man worships God only because of fear. He needs something. That's why sometimes he worships a tree, sometimes he worships a stone. It is because of fear that one worships mountains, forests, rivers, lakes and forests and trees. Takes refuge in him. Mahatma Buddha sent one of his supremely conscious disciples, Maudgalayana, to Sravasti to see Agnidatta in order to bring him to the path of enlightenment. When Maudgalayan went, Agnidatta did not even ask to sit. Maudgalyana then had to spend the night on a sand dune. There was a cobra, who was protecting Maudgalyana by taking out his hood. Agnidatta then asked Mahatma Buddha what kind of miracle it was. Buddha said think in another way, a bigger miracle happened than this, a man could not recognize while the snake recognized. The animal recognizes, the snake knows, but the man is so influenced by selfishness and greed that he does not want to recognize anything. The highest refuge, freedom from sorrow, the light of truth and drowning in the ocean of knowledge. The one who took refuge after awakening, the one who searched for the ultimate source of awakening, which is the ultimate refuge.

Life and nature are governed by laws that man cannot change. The sooner we accept this, the easier it will be for us to find inner peace.

Epictetus

Health depends on the rhythmicity between two breaths

Why does disease come in our life? What is its sponsorship? People believe that illness acts as a catalyst. Illness disrupts the order of our daily lives. It realizes the limitations of the individual. Makes a person realize that he should decide his priorities. After all there is an end to this life, so the message of that end is received through illness. Illness is a medium, to arrange life in the right order. Departure from life begins with illness. The question is what is disease? Reaction to any drug. That is, there is no effect of the medicine given for the disease. On the contrary, its response is to have pain, pain and anger in the body.

Some diseases of life remain with us for life. We pass through it again and again and each time a new story is encountered. If a grandparent or maternal grandparent has a disease, there is a genetic possibility of passing that disease on to a grandchild, grandchild, or another family member. This is known when it intensely leaves its effect on the body. Sometimes illness also becomes a medium to increase our knowledge. Through this it is taught that we will continue to grow, grow, even if our body ends with life. The health of a person is not related to the body, but to the soul. Disease prevention is related to body and mind. In spite of illness one can give the appearance of health because in such a state one establishes oneself in the realm of God beyond the pain and suffering of the senses. The Prana that is within us decays due to our decision rather than disease. Have read - the diagnosis of lifethreatening diseases pushes us directly into the subjective world. Those people who wander from place to place for the treatment of diseases, they are afraid to look within themselves. Somewhere deep down they are afraid of facing their inferior and unworthy self. But this rarely happens. Soul is our birthright. And deep down everyone is beautiful.

Man forgets everything in pain, but I saw my mother forgetting pain in God. Whether it is a matter of pilgrimage or yagya-havan or what else any occasion of worship. She would have forgotten the disease. Illness is a time of trial, but saw it changing the clock. Often she does not allow her own physical pain to dominate in the path of God's grace. Illness and suffering never lead us to reject life. If the person does not want it from his spiritual form, then even this suffering cannot dominate our mind and body. The lives of Mahatma Buddha, Shakaracharya, Swami Vivekananda, and Raman Maharshi are examples of this. Swami Vivekananda is the best example of endurance in illness. Life wants perfection and we live on the surface. Human is the only creature in the universe, who violates the established rules and regulations of nature. Even in illness, only humans eat, and no other creature. Health is a game of life energy ie consciousness. There is only one energy which keeps trees, animals and other living beings healthy, so why can't humans be healthy? Dr. Bernie Siegel, a surgeon from England, has written a book: Peace, Love and Healing. In this they establish only one thing that a happy and positive person is healthy and gets free from any disease soon. Now modern science also believes that the body is a flowing current and the mind is a subtler aspect of the body itself.

In homeopathy, as the potency of the medicine increases, the proportion of the medicine in it decreases. It tells that staying healthy is not related to medicine or medicine. Medicine only helps to control or prevent the disease. But the body itself makes itself healthy, otherwise the doctor would not say that the body is not responding to the medicine. Hahnemann, the father of homeopathy, believed that mental illness is the cause of physical illness. The three defects of all diseases are Psora, Sycosis and Syphilis. There are infinite seeds of jealousy, malice, lust, anger, greed lying in human beings, which seek an opportunity to become vocal. As per the disorder in the mind, the same diseases start arising. Health is a state of well-being and our mind is always talking to us, provided we can listen to it.

Illness is a story. The more you hear, know and understand, the more you get connected with it. The themes of its story are pain, sorrow, hope, agony, wound, hunger, desire and health. These stories are basically the story of life. Have some patience and listen calmly to the meaning of the story. The origin of every story becomes clearer when we connect with the Supreme

Being. From the story of that ultimate authority. His story also appeared in various forms. If a sick person does not want to, we cannot keep him alive even by giving oxygen, we cannot cure him even by giving medicines and we cannot save him even by surgery, then the result of these external measures is zero. Life is just between two breaths. And whether or not to take this breath is dependent on our Pranashakti i.e. the entity of supreme power i.e. Atma or Paramatma.

The most important aspect of courage is to have the determination to do something in advance, and this is possible only when, without choosing the path where they lead, they move in the direction where there is no path.

Ralph Waldo Emerson

Tears are the climax of compassion

It is difficult to make a man laugh, but it is easy to make him cry. That's why the tear drops are small, but the story is big. Most of the discussions and writings in literature were on love, so the flow of tears would be a little less than love. *Aansu is a poem by Jaishankar Prasad.* In which he writes – The deep pain that was there was like a memory in the brain. Hope came to rain in the form of tears in a bad day. Nowadays the complexity of life has reduced the sensitivity due to which crying is a bit difficult. But social behaviour demands that tears should be shed.

Charles Dickens wrote a novel on the concern of poverty, which is named Oliver Twist. In this, a character Bumble says – Crying clears the lungs, washes the face, exercises the eyes and reduces anger. Apart from this, crying makes a person light, reduces mental burden and connects oneself with spirituality. Tears are not related to any particular person, society or caste and religion. This is for everyone. It is generally believed that tears come out only in pain and suffering, which is not correct. Tears come out of the eyes even on happiness and achievement. If we increase the happiness of man by laughing, then we share his sorrow by shedding tears in sorrow. That's why it has been said that whether one is involved in happiness or not, one should be involved in one's sorrow. Salty tears play an important role in improving life.

The glory of tears is unique. She washes away the biggest problems in a jiffy. This intensifies the person's experience. Men shed fewer tears than women. They keep kneeling inside. Men think that crying is a sign of weakness. That's why men refrain from crying, while crying is better for health. The outbreak of disease in a person who cries is less than the person who does not cry. Tears play an important role in keeping our internal system healthy.

What is tear? Tears are the fluid that comes out of the eye canals, which are made of a mixture of water and salt. It is also beneficial for the eyes. It prevents drying of the eye. Tears also help in cleaning and disinfecting the eye. If there is life, fear and tears are a natural process. It is not right to stop or suppress it. Naturally the natural process must be controlled. Tears are like a safety valve in our body. so stop the tears No, let it flow. When I used to be sad in childhood, tears used to come in my eyes. On those occasion's mother used to say that go and wash your eyes with plenty of water. Sorrows used to end with a few splashes of water. But today we have grown up, so the sorrows don't go away at all! There is a song in the movie Anari – *Markar bhi kisi ki aansoo mein muskarayenge, jeena isi ka naam hai.* Memories are closely related to tears. Its story is long.

To fulfil every desire in life, we have to work and if we do not get success in it, we suffer from anxiety, sorrow, dissatisfaction and frustration. Tears are the extreme culmination of such feelings. The specialty of *Chhayavadi* poets was that they considered happiness and sorrow to be the eyesore of life. Prasadji's poem is - Human life is on the altar, separation is the end of meeting. Happiness and sorrow both will dance, it is a game of eyes and mind.

Nothing is purer than tears. No big prayer. People have known one form of tears as sorrow. There is another form of bliss. When we see crying, it seems that there will be pain, there will be sorrow. Tears flow when an emotion becomes excessive, it flows. If happiness is too much, if joy is too much, then it flows away with tears. It is a process of balancing. Sadness has nothing to do with tears. Otherwise someone would have stopped all this. Sorrow is associated with tears. Tears of sorrow Cry if you die, cry if you are sad. We did not make tears an occasion for joy.

A time will come when there will be very few people who cry in sorrow. Now crying is a sign of weakness. When no one cries in sorrow, he is called sensible, called a man. People are stopping crying in sorrow. Such a man himself will turn to stone. The best man cries in joy and the worst man cries in sorrow. Eyes will be filled with tears on seeing the blossoming flower, sometimes tears will be drowned on seeing the stars in the sky. Crying seeing children playing, crying by making green leaves of trees, clouds in the sky as instruments is life. When you have to cry, you have to learn the art of crying in joy, so that you don't have to cry in sorrow. Connecting tears with joy is the key to life. Only then will death be filled with the joy of life at the moment.

It is also true of the whole experience of life that whatever happens, happens in our innermost being. If you see beauty in a star, it happens in your inner self. When the eye is wet, then only compassion comes. Only then music starts, otherwise who sees the deity in the stone. If the tears are of gratitude, if they are of compassion, if they are of deep poetry, then it is a different matter. Crying will end the doubt. Truth will be faced in life.

The whole earth rests on the strength of truth and there is an unshakable rule of creation that whatever means it is obtained, it is also protected by the same means. Also, the collection of things related to truth can also be done through truth only.

Mahatma Gandhi

It is necessary for the best to excel the consciousness

Our whole life has been a part of the crowd. Be it a crowd of ideas, or ideals of organizations or individuals. Nothing innovative happens in the consciousness of most people. He makes a roadmap, and that roadmap is just to follow the crowd. In education, children do the same, which is more craze among the youth. In the family, children follow their parents or their elders or friends. This iteration happens in every case. Either wrong and right qualities or habits are adopted. It is not a question of right or wrong. The question is why the feeling of doing something new does not come in our consciousness. And if it doesn't come, from where can we give the best? How can we be great? An example. Harvard Business School has now decided to focus more on ethical education and teamwork, removing the case study approach from its syllabus. This change is meant to create capable and character-strong leaders. Not a leader with connections and credentials. This change came to the attention of business schools only after the 2008 recession.

Many business school pedagogies in the western world shift the focus from "knowing" (facts, frameworks, principles) to "doing" (capabilities and techniques) and "being" (values, attitudes and beliefs). Is. There is also more focus on thinking with it. For example, how to think in critical times. Topics such as serving in NGOs, leadership development, participation in cultural festivals, research, improving living conditions are being given place in the curriculum. Garden visits and dentist visits are prioritized among school children so that they don't have to explain the goodness of the environment or the benefits of brushing their teeth properly. Children are being taught to value what they have and to face life with ease.

There is no need of philosophy in the life we are living at present. Knowing or solving math or management formulas is not enough. With this, efficiency and skill are necessary for success. And for this a change in mind set and thinking is necessary. We have to understand and apply the benefits of patience, perseverance and consistent hard work in our daily life. We have to be more positive and acceptable so that we can stand firm even in confusion. Instead of focusing on the problem, it is better to accept the challenge and overcome it. In fact every problem provides an opportunity for us. If we can use this opportunity, the situation will be our slave. In the second phase, the art of keeping oneself peaceful, pleasant and happy has to be learned. It is more relevant to learn that no matter what the situation or crisis, we can keep our calm nature. He will not leave. Only a person who is in a calm state thinks in a practical way. They are capable of taking the right decisions. And in any situation, don't let the escapist attitude come. In the third stage for success, we have to explore independently and think clearly. After this, work will have to be done in the direction of implementing the efforts without any hesitation. This is a difficult task, because from childhood our psyche, our thinking system is based on truth and honesty. Creativity is a mental and emotional attitude that observes all kinds of knowledge and experience in a new perspective. This helps in the emergence of new ideas. Leads the way in innovative process planning and invention of the best service and product, to serve humanity in a better way. Creation is possible only when we think. It is a combination of innovation, innovation, creation and right assessment of the future at the same time.

In childhood, we had heard from our mother that - Son, live properly. Do not walk bending down, keep the neck straight and the chest high. New research suggests that what you think is what your body postures are. If the body is loose, then there will be no mental acuity. The fast-moving body will think in the same way. People who adopt a more vigorous posture during daily life and keep their bodies in shape not only feel more powerful, but are also able to keep things more under control and are able to overcome problems such as stress. There are bad body posture not only creates a wrong image of you in the minds of others, but can also weaken you physically. Being creative means finding new ways to do anything. The basic need of creativity is trust. The belief is that this work can be done in a new way. As soon as you believe, the mind starts working for you. Remember average people always tease in new ways.

The law of nature is the law of life. If it is deeply analysed, it will be found that the law of nature is contradictory to the law of ending one's own life by a person. To do so is to defy the natural law of possibilities of improvement in life. Human life is not a commodity. Therefore, instead of ending one's life, one should try to make the situation tolerable till the end.

Immanuel Kant

Should be living the best life, but where is the family?

Family is an important institution for human life. A person needs a family to listen to his words. Family is necessary to share sorrows and happiness, to laugh, to speak. Apart from mother, father, brother, sister, there is an unbreakable relation of relatives in the family. When necessary, he went to his mother as per his wish, talked to his father. Share your feelings with brother and sister. One gets the first lesson of education from the family. If there is a family, then there is a feeling of dignity and morality. Etiquette, ethos and thought-behaviour are learned from time to time. The institution that joins in happiness and shares sorrow is the family. The family becomes an ally in bringing harmony in the family and taking life forward despite all the ifs and buts.

Today is the era of nuclear family, where everything has to be done by oneself, it has to be felt by oneself. No one here to share or share. This is the market, where there is crowd. Everyone is standing, but alone. The market itself determines the definition of limits, responsibilities and actions. Whereas in Indian life this work was given to the family. The members of the family were expected to co-operate with the members of the family institution. Make mutual relations and contacts.

A family is not made by living with some people, it has a strong thread of relationship. There is an unbreakable bond of cooperation. Today families are breaking, so human beings are also breaking. Increase in suicide, stress, discord, violence, mental anxiety, crime etc. is an indication of the fact that there is no limit. There is no one to tell you the limits. Let us control anger, not such a father. To communicate compassion, it is not the mother who teaches. Not brother and sister, who makes one realize the ethos, thoughts and behaviour. Exercise restraint in the time of decision, such education is not given in our school. Failure is also a part of life. It is not a teacher who tells such things. Who will tell, there will not be a smooth road to reach the top in life. Somewhere there will be footpaths, and somewhere roads will have to be made. Have to find the lighthouse. There is no straight path to a successful life. The way to reach the summit will be crooked. In such a situation, one victory is not enough. Who will teach this? We will become engineers and doctors by solving maths and science questions, but who will tell what is required to reach the pinnacle of this profession. The present generation is happy living an average life with success. Whereas man should live the best life with failure. One may be restless, a failure, but one should strive for excellence, and such should be the aim of life. This lesson comes from the family! But where is the family?

It is repeatedly said that Rome and Greece have disappeared. Still India is alive. If so, why and how? In fact, behind India's continuity and energy is the strength of the family. Even today Indian families are left. Are not scattered, so India is special. In times of throes of joy and sorrow, loneliness and emotional breakdown, the family is the first to give strength. Music and mourning of birth and death are also celebrated at the family level. That's why the person of India does not break down, but fights and struggles with the circumstances. Doesn't get mentally ill easily because the family supports him.

The role of mother and father in the family is indelible. This thing has been getting importance in Indian life for hundreds of years, but western civilization has understood the importance of father and mother in the last hundred years. For this reason, festivals like Father's Day and Mother's Day are now being promoted in western countries. They are now realizing what their children are losing without the institution of family. The role of parents in the family is social based on empathy. The importance of these institutions has been understood in the West, but Father's Day and Mother's Day have been used to remember the importance of these institutions. And thus the whole issue has been made a marketing event. This is not right. The role of the father in the family is sometimes that of a friend, sometimes a teacher, sometimes a leader, sometimes a protector and a trouble-shooter. Similarly, the role of mother is sometimes that of teacher, mother, motivator, loving, guiding, advisor etc.

This is the era of management and management is discussed in everything. Time Management, Office Management, Task Management, Boss and Employee Management etc etc. Now the matter has gone ahead and the matter of managing relationships has also come up. Now the principles governing the relationship between family or husband and wife are sought and explained. These days a book by my Adriana George is very much discussed - How to Manage Your Spouse? This book has also been translated into French and German languages. In India, the relationship between husband and wife is not yet managed. Husband-wife or family coordination takes place in the Indian environment. Happiness and sorrow are shared in this family. In case of emergency, everyone works together to solve the problem. Here in the family, only dedication towards each other keeps the relationships unbreakable. There is no meaning of managing in a relationship, if the feeling of managing comes in the family too, then the relationship and life will lose its spontaneity and naturalness. In an Indian family, husband and wife give so much to each other in life that there is no counting of it. If its mathematics is started, then the sweetness and sensitivity of Indian culture will end.

Today, in place of family, nuclear family, instead of home, family and harmony and interdependent society, opportunistic selfish society is taking place. When a child is not taught about culture, tradition and ideals, then from where will he think about the nation? Where families are united, children feel the special love of God in their parents. And growing up, they give the same love and faith to their country.

The rainbow that seems distant and unfamiliar but close is the clarity of life. Actually the colors of life are not hidden in the rainbow but in its search.

D H Lawrence

Recognition of superiority depends only on the acceptance

What is the problem of present society? We are the only best ! No one more than us. What we do should become the standard. Trying to set yourself up as a role model. While it is an established belief that excellence is identified by the outsider. A person cannot declare himself. If we are good, then society will accept us. In this technological age, where distances have reduced, the same person has also shrunk. His thoughts, feelings and relationships have also become narrow. The person may be tall, but he has become short. That's why he does more than expected, and even if there is no neglect, the expectation is breaking him. Expectation is a mite, which keeps on licking us from inside. Today the child does not know what to do? What to become but the parents are under full pressure. They want to make the child an engineer, a doctor. Less than 10 GPA in 10th is not acceptable. 90% must come in 11th. Just the expectation of the parents, while it becomes the cause of neglect for the children. In every family, in every company, a person expects respect, money, comfort, promotion. One is dying in the hope of becoming a great man. No one has time to think about life. Coaching institutes in every city are like production machines or 100% guarantee of success.

If the cause of neglect is expectation, then the cause of expectation is neglect. Perhaps both complement each other. This is a person who can neither escape from neglect nor can remove expectation from his mind. Both are the hindering elements of the development of the individual, society and the country. Expectation destroys us from inside, spoils us. Neglect weakens us from outside. This is an external attack. If expectation is a self-contained feeling, then neglect is a dependent thought. When the essential desire of a person becomes unlimited, then it brings a flood of aspirations. Due to this, a person makes himself subordinate to jealousy, malice and ego. When we are sad, we shed tears. Let's clean ourselves. Makes it pure. When we are angry, we hurt others. They also subject themselves to various impulses and passions. In sorrow we are free, whereas in anger we are united. Expectation is anger and neglect is sorrow. Why is it that we begin to feel that my dear, I Hey co-workers are ignoring us. Running away from us. We ourselves are becoming lonely. Doesn't a person's indifference and arrogance become the reason for neglect and expectation?

What is life? Admission in IIT, desire for IAS, yearning to become General Manager, lots of money, big position, lots of status, and prestige. Can't we ever sit and think that apart from the toppers, other people also live well in the world. Happiness can be felt even in poverty, without expectation. Juice is also found in roti and greens. It is necessary to live life instead of falling into the trap of expectation and neglect in the form of right-wrong, truth and falsehood. Sometimes deliberate mistakes are also better than those truths, which turn into lies at some stage of life's journey. Nor is there a limit to magnificence, and no established pinnacle of prosperity. Despite this, the stubbornness to be called the best and the yearning to reach the peak of prosperity have destroyed life. Our attitudes have changed, our meanings have changed. A few days ago, the way we used to see ourselves and the society around us, that vision is no more. Our society has changed. The face of India changed. This is the era of the market. Everything is seen from the point of view of business. Matter, feeling, labour and your body too. Now everyone wants to be rich, and for that the basic mantra is- the wisdom of the tradesman and the daring of the brother.

A man becomes Purushottam when there is a continuous ascent of consciousness. For that we always remained active. Consciousness should be filled with lofty feelings of life, accept that which is better for the society than the beloved. Let the mind be devoted to a great goal beyond duality. Build a character free from attachment and hatred. In Indian philosophy, the soul has been called pure, but if the body of five elements becomes pure, pure and supernatural, then the life of a person turns into Purushottam. The ascension of consciousness is not easy. Body has its own science, nature has different effect on life. Purity of soul is a journey of a different path. How to conduct life between the demands of the body and the influence of nature? This was shown by Shri Ram. Since childhood. Living among brothers encourage them. Salvation of Ahilya, conversation with Parshuram, sight of Sita for the first time, observance of decorum during food in marriage. After all, how did Shri Ram become the pinnacle of dignity? It's a research topic! This dignity which is the demand of present India. The call of the society remains. There has become a need for a balance between market and enjoyment. Shri Ram is remembered. Why? India's identity, its spiritual heritage is now trapped in the maze of fear and indulgence. If it is to be saved, then Ram is the only solution.

If a person yearns for something valuable, Idam motivates him to adopt any means for its attainment. Ego tells to wait till proper conditions are created to achieve the object, but Paraham tells to achieve the goal keeping in mind the morality.

Sigmund Freud

It is necessary to separate oneself from karma for freedom

When we look at the deeds of our life on this criterion, it will be known that most of our deeds were the result of influences. Thus freedom in true sense is very rarely found. Often people think or say that they are independent. But someone or the other definitely has an influence on their mind, thoughts and consciousness. It is most difficult to get free from this chain of influence. No one, whether knowledgeable or intellectual, is free from this. Even if there is no effect, the deeds of past lives inspire or influence us. Thus there is always some or the other effect on our freedom. The status of a person in the society is the level of his consciousness. Whatever the individual's consciousness says, he does what is determined by his social existence. Consciousness is determined by social status, but it is not the only one.

Everyone has attachments. There are some trends. The person remains engrossed in this attachment and tendency. This trend will sometimes be of meaning, sometimes of love. Sometimes it will be of fame and sometimes of glory. Every person's life keeps on swinging between these attachments and tendencies and in the end when the person gets tired, then he comes to know that it was hypnosis. The way to get out of this hypnosis is also with consciousness or discrimination. If a person accepts poverty, he can be the master of higher consciousness. But even if a rich man is not satisfied with his riches, he cannot be the master of higher consciousness. It depends on how much he is in control of his self. what is his freedom? How much the conscience is able to guide his thinking, he remains under credit or love. Accepting knowledge and practicing absolute, then a person can create a stream different from the mainstream of society like Kabir, Gandhi or JP. These persons or others like it were able to do so because they were not influenced by the society or any other relative thing. One eternal truth resides at the root of all things, ideas, concepts and beliefs in the world. This truth is beyond the boundaries of space and time and whose recognition does not depend on the discretion or intelligence of a person.

In fact the green man is a rude hermit. Humans are good by nature. But it is this consciousness, his independence, which motivates him to take the path of wrong or right. In the early period of creation, the conscience of human was more pure, in which it got mixed due to the influence of time? All Realization of one's own and alienation has happened and is happening because of wealth. Just as it cannot be decided that a farmer's son will be a farmer or a slave's son a slave. Similarly, to decide that a person cannot be under self is wrong. Since every man is born free and is his own master. In such a situation, no person has the right to mortgage his freedom or consciousness by subjecting himself to any pretext or other elements of acceptance. And after doing this, that person cannot blame the society. Yes, it is the responsibility of the society that the person should remain free and independent.

In such a situation the question again arises where is our freedom? How free are we? Most people are like lifeless furniture. Weak and dilapidated due to attachment and tendency. The only way to be free from the bondage of this karma and freedom is to connect yourself with that supreme consciousness. Integrate yourself with the whole soul. Believing we are in bondage stunts our growth. When we think like this, then we will not give anything new to life to the world. To give something, you have to free yourself. Civilization, nationality, society and family and any other influencing factors. Even if it is a bond of good deeds? Vedic sages said after wandering in the depths of consciousness - *Shivodham!* I am free He separated himself from Karma. Only such people can become ideals of society and life. Be it Buddha or Kabir. Gandhi or Tagore. The actions of those who are independent are not influenced by anything other than knowledge. Mahatma Gandhi was such an independent human being. When he went to England and went to meet the king and queen there, he did not wear a suit according to the custom there. He welcomed them in simple rustic dhoti and shawl. They were enjoying great freedom. On whom there was no bond of material attachment of civilization. True freedom means doing what you want to do. Only by being implemented with knowledge and discretion.

Swami Vivekananda says that Karma is the eternal declaration of human freedom – our thoughts, our words and our deeds are the threads by which we weave a web around us. Each of our actions creates such energy, which gives a similar response. We reap what we sow. the knowledge of Advaita is the inspiration of freedom. His ignorance is bondage. If a person is mentally bound, then freedom cannot be exercised, as happened in India after independence. Rabindranath Tagore in the fourteenth section of Santiniketan said regarding freedom that 'the Supreme is also both free and unfree. Brahman is bound by its truth and free from its bliss. We can enjoy the fullness of our freedom only when we accept the bondage of truth.

Through the pursuit of truth one can attain freedom. The search for freedom begins with the struggle for the existence of the individual and in this sequence the individual also takes the search for truth as a supporting element. Human freedom is the basis of ancient Indian thought. This was the reason why the goal of human life was kept attainment of *Satchitananda* (The Truth, the goodness and the happiness) instead of seeing God. Man was freed from all bondages by saying *Aham Brahmamasmi* and he was considered to be the creator of his destiny. Freedom is not just physical or mental. Many people think that they are free because they can think and speak. You can move as per your wish. But this is not freedom. They are in bondage, chained to their nature and dormant tendencies, like sleepwalking people.

Even in the West, freedom was interpreted according to time and situation. Till the medieval period, the meaning of freedom has been understood by the free and pleasant environment for human life in the society. In modern times, Machiavelli also made a difference between freedom and slavery, then talked about the desire for this pleasant environment, which was not available to the public during the era of autocratic rulers. After individual freedom, it was discussed in the West as the freedom of political parties and institutions, obstacles coming in the way of freedom. Considering freedom, negative freedom and positive freedom were talked about. In the first type of freedom, a person was considered autonomous, while in the second type of freedom, some restrictions were said, so that public welfare work could be done. Against this definition came the idea of Marxist freedom. This idea sacrifices the freedom of the individual himself for the equal development of the individual. It is in favour of giving that much freedom so that all round development of all individuals is possible.

Freedom is a thirst that excites everyone. But what is the true form of freedom? Negative freedom is the desire to be free from something, object or person. To be a painter, to use the freedom to pursue one's hobby is positive freedom. In such freedom, a person is creative, who gets interest in building. There is another freedom called pure freedom in which personal liberation is the goal. The word freedom itself explains it. Self's system? That is, the technique by which a person can open the door to his inner wealth. The one who has got such tantra remains free even in the midst of all the bondages. Can't go It cannot be reasoned with. It cannot be theorized. Nor can it be discussed, or understood. God can only be lived.

Mehar Baba

God is the name of complete happiness in life

Paramahansa Yogananda, one of the world's great spiritual teachers, writes in his book Man's Continual Search that mankind is engaged in a constant search for "something else" in which it hopes to find complete and infinite happiness. For those special souls who have sought and found God, the search is now over: God is "something else". In our life this "something else" i.e. the search for completeness is always going on, but it is rarely complete. We should understand that when a flower blooms in its ultimate beauty, a stone appears in the form of a deity or a voice touches the heart. This highest peak is God. The name of this supreme excellence is God.

It was discovered thousands of years ago by the Vedic sages that it is not possible to enjoy inner or ultimate happiness through physical happiness. No matter how much external prosperity there is, there is no permanent happiness. Happiness is the creation of your mind. The beauty of our most precious object which we are seeing with our eyes, vanishes as soon as the thoughts are removed from that object. We are all thirsty for joy, for peace and for happiness. And the truth is that throughout life they keep running to get material things-gold, food, clothes, money and position. Even in this race, the feeling remains that happiness is being enjoyed. This attitude persists that life's fulfilment is being found, but life ends little by little like Alexander. In the race of constant desire and its fulfilment, we remain two steps behind our goal. Hunger is infinite, thirst is infinite. But the most amazing thing is that behind all the desires there remains the yearning to finally attain God. Be it the ultimate glory or the ultimate opulence, all forms are the form of God. Wherever excellence is seen, there is truth, there is Shiva and manifestation of beauty.

There is an interesting story. A small child wanted to meet God. He prayed, God you talk to me. Just then a bird chirped but the child did not listen. He again asked God to talk to me. Then there was a loud roar from the sky. The child again did not pay attention. He again told God that I want to see you. Then a beautiful star shone in the sky. But the child's attention was elsewhere. After this the child shouted. O God, show me a miracle. Then suddenly a squirrel came in front of him but that child could not even know this. Now the child was tired. He started crying and said Lord you touch us so that I can feel. Then God came down and sat on the hand, but the child removed the beautiful butterfly sitting on the hand. And went towards his home. The lesson of this story is that God is everything. He comes before us in different forms, sometimes with sorrow, sometimes with happiness, sometimes with wealth and sometimes with poverty. We ourselves do not recognize them. Not even in opulence and not even in a state of scarcity.

Our Gurudev Yogananda says that all paths lead to God, because ultimately there is no other place for the soul to go. Everything came out of God and it must go back to him. The beauty of God, His truth and His form of Shiva are hidden in all the creations of this creation. The power of attraction of God's creations continuously attracts us to attain that supreme happiness. It is the attraction of God and the ultimate happiness contained in it that we keep ourselves busy in the constant search for "something else". And we keep ourselves away from the supreme happiness by getting caught in the clutches of the worldly. Osho says at one place in his Gita discourse that whenever the great God comes in front of us, our petty ego gets restless. We can worship the dead God, but it is difficult to identify the living God.

Our problem is our thinking. Wherever something touches excellence, attains supreme glory, there one starts getting glimpses of God. The consciousness of God first manifested itself in stones or in inert mineral substances. After this, the plants become sensitive. After this it appears in the world of animals and birds with self-consciousness. God manifests in man in the highest forms through his consciousness, reason, life force and conscience. But we do not use our discretion, consciousness and reasoning power. We don't try to see by lifting our eyes that high. We are ordinary, so how can we think extraordinary. For this it is necessary to change the vision. Nietzsche has said that if there is a God, I will continue to deny it, until I too sit at the same height.

In the words of Yogananda, God has been calling everything from eternity in a soft voice, to rest in himself. To experience that supreme happiness. For this they invite through smiling flowers, serious mountains, chilling oceans, cheerful winds. Spiritual sages say that those who can hear can still hear Krishna's flute on the banks of the Yamuna. Those who can hear, can still hear the songs of Radha in Vrindavan. But those eyes are needed, those ears are needed. That feeling of Ramakrishna is needed who sees Maa Kali in the idol, but his supremely knowledgeable disciples are not able to see Bhagwati. Our senses pull the human soul towards material pleasure and the outer world. Human happiness and He searches for happiness where he can never get eternal happiness. For this it is necessary to travel within and merge oneself in supreme happiness.

Relinquishment of actions is not renunciation. Similarly, no one becomes a sannyasin even by saying that he is a sannyasin. The sense of unity of the soul and the divine in samadhi is called sannyas.

Maitreyi Upanishad

The world of flowers makes life meaningful

As all existence is interrelated, so is life. Be it childhood or old age. It is the condensed form of our thinking. If life is meaningful and blossoms like a flower, then every stage is happy and creative. What is flower? The one who has blossomed is a flower. This is the sign of the meaning of life. Makes life meaningful. If old age is meaningful, we blossom like a flower. Then life too will tell a story, like a flower. It has been told in the scriptures that God is a flower, so we made the goddesses, gods and all Buddhas sit on the flower. Osho says that the one who kept on worshiping the tree, got stuck. The one who accepted the flower as everything, he also did not get the ultimate. The one who becomes one with its fragrance, he has understood the truth.

The stubbornness and ability to stand at least in convenience and spread the fragrance of happiness, prayer and enthusiasm and enthusiasm in a short life span are only within the control of flowers. For the first time in this world the first flower blossomed 114 million years ago. After this revolutionary event in the life of plants, our earth was covered with a soft and fragrant substance called flower. This fascination with flowers in forests and groves has continued since then. Whatever the season, flowers tell a story. Whether it is the winter season or the hot afternoon of Jeth, flowers always tell something. The hum of the bumblebee, the fifth note of the cuckoo, the fragrance of life, the satisfaction of hunger and the infinite journey of smell. Where I work, the plants of Dahlia, Chrysanthemum, Rose, Sunflower, Marigold, Lotus, Beganbelia etc. and flowers of various colours bloom on them. I see that they neither need much water nor much care. Within a few days of planting in the pot, the buds begin to bud. It is an occasion for the flower to blossom and through it blossom the atmosphere. Whenever I see them or flowers in any garden, the flowers blooming all around look like smiling faces. And a voice rises from the heart that I wish! How nice it would be if each sad and troubled face could get a colour of their choice.

Living among these flowers and gardens for the last many years, I have learned that - the name of life goes on, morning and evening. There will be stages of childhood, youth, old age and retirement in life. Just have to go on, keep blooming. Life has to be made a fragrant prayer. This prayer teaches us the mantra of being selfless. He gives the art of sacrificing his everything for others. In autumn, flowers, leaves and stems all struggle to keep themselves alive. Trying to survive and keep in low adaptability. Their goal is happiness and fragrance. Life is also like this. The message of flowers is to feel the fragrance of life present in the midst of every disease. The feeling of a flower is most alive. You name a flower. His form will float before the eyes. There will be a fragrance in the breath. Its wave of coolness will touch the heart. Life is also like this. The whole of nature is intertwined with a web of invisible relationships. And the dense texture and fine existence of these nature's inner beliefs binds all life to itself. No different. Neither childhood nor old age. Flowers make us know the interrelationship of life.

Flowers have inspired innumerable artists, poets and mystics. Jesus Christ says contemplate the flowers and learn from them how to live. Once, during a silent sermon before his disciples, Mahatma Buddha held a flower in his hand and looked at it. After some time, a monk Mahakashyap present there started smiling. The things about flowers are unique. The world of their fragrance is unique. The colour is attractive and the juice is like a pot of nectar. They blossom, they blossom. They smell, chirp, together they call us near. Flowers are such an object, which is liked by children, youth and elders. When flowers look good, then why can't we take the message of beauty, karma, fragrance from them? When it comes to beauty in life, tuberose flower comes to the fore. The night queen, who feels like her queen at night, may be tired throughout the day, but as soon as the darkness sets in, her intoxicating and refreshing atmosphere engulfs her. Such should be old age. Full of freshness and sweetness. To make the night as attractive as the day, the night falling from the flowers of Harsingar (A type of flower) is something else. It teaches us how to live for the sake of others by forgetting ourselves all the time.

The basis of life is aggregate. Unity. Childhood is separate, old age is not separate. Marigold flower gives the sense of a set. He says that nature has only one basis. If you want to know and understand this, then look at the marigold. How to manifest your entire existence with one base! This is the reason why many times when the flowers are less, the single marigold flower is converted into many petals and offered at the feet of the gods. Like flowers, the mind creates its own world. Sometimes separately and sometimes in combination. The very thing about the lotus flower is unique. Mahadevi Verma calls the lotus flower Asha Kamal – Punk

J bud. Silent eyes burning with the sun. Soft pug shivering in the water. On which fast do you fast and do not get deceived by sorrow and happiness. Lotus is an example of transparent relationship in life. If it blooms on the land outside the water, then the rose means Sthalkamal and the flower that blooms on the top of the mountain is called Brahmakamal, which fulfils all our wishes. And sunflowers can make any sad heart blossom. It looks like a sunflower garden, small suns have come up. Whenever I am bored with work, I look at the sunflower flower, which gives us moments of glee by facing the sun. We should illuminate life with such small suns.

In whose destruction is there salvation? Only in the destruction of the mind. Who has no fear at all? In free. Who is the biggest thorn? It's your stupidity. Who is worthy of worship? Guru, deity and old man.

Adi Shankaracharya

If you are going wrong in life then look back

What is the greatest gift in the world? Keeping yourself in the present Make yourself active every moment. Considering the present English word as aviation and expanding it, then it would mean – Prime Resource Emerging Silently Evolving Now Today. That is, the fundamental potential is being expanded and expressed silently today and every moment. When we are fully with a moment, we should act in such a way that it gives us the joy of achievement, well-being and contentment.

Every moment is silently coming to us by itself. We have no idea of its power because it comes to us quietly and freely. A single moment has millions of possibilities attached to it. This gives us opportunity, hope and adaptability, so that we can develop and expand ourselves. You will be able to understand the power of every moment of time only when you think, think and act accordingly. When we think, then only we will be able to decide our priorities and make an action plan accordingly. What we do? Live in every moment, and be won. No idea, no plan. As a result, despair, failure and fear pervade. Because of our procrastination attitude, the present is not utilized. As soon as we avoid the present, we invite disease, which engulfs us.

What is the current Present does not mean beyond past and future. Present is nothing. This time does not happen. When we think in time and moment, it will be future or past. Not current. Therefore, the meaning of present is to live life fully conscious. Apart from this life is nothing else. The time we are living in is important. And the environment and the person who is around. That is what is important. Enough. We like the past the most. Why? It takes us to the pleasant world of feelings and thoughts. We feel good when suddenly some good thoughts come, only then we are moved by some sad incident and go into the ocean of sorrow. Is this the goodness of ghost? Past means. Post means Poignant Association Standing Testimony, that is, to stand the test of life with the thought and association of duality.

During family discussion we say – those days were so good! That's why the younger ones of the house will be surprised and ask what is good in it? No mobile, computer, no internet, flood, drought and various diseases. Neither electricity nor any smell of democracy. How were those good days? Then our answer is that where is the meaning of family now? At that time the family consisted of uncle, aunt, grandfather, grandmother and all the children together. The whole village used to come in the bigger family. At that time there was freshness and simplicity in marriage, studies, food and life. Life was simple, as well as sweet. Not as heavy as today. There was self-respect and determination, which proved itself during the examination period, did not break like today. Since the good old days, we proceed on the basis of our feelings and imaginations. We install love and compassion for the family, as our parents used to do in the past. Life cannot become meaningful without forgetting the past. It should always be used in the foundation of the present. It teaches. It forms the base. Provides juice to life.

As night is necessary with day, similarly past is necessary with present and future.

Tomorrow is a long journey for most. In such a situation, the future is as far away as light years. We express happiness by living in the present. If it is more than this, then by turning the pages of the past, we are satisfied. When we are doing this, we do not think that the future which we have left as imagination is here, we just have to change the attitude of looking at it. Visualizing the future at the individual level gives us positive confidence. It gives us time, opportunity and learns to use the experience to better ourselves. We can take advantage of this only when we will use the coming tomorrow with a strong will, faith and natural thoughts. For this it is necessary that first we think about what we want to happen tomorrow. What are our long term goals? What do we want to achieve immediately?

If we do not understand the importance of time? If we don't assess the future, those who wish for natural change will not be possible. Science and technology has accelerated the pace of change so much that it affects us more intensely than we think. If we fall in the clutches of time, then we will not be able to adjust our demand according to time. In the era we live in, we cannot ignore change. the future is upon us Comes at a faster pace that one has to either accept, adjust with the pace of life or make oneself move with its pace. The change of the future is so subtle, efficient and non-communicative that it is challenging the entire social change. Social beliefs are collapsing, our thoughts and ideas are gaining momentum, affecting the psychological structure. In such a situation, it would be wise to accept the future changes and adjust them according to the present. This is an opportunity as well as a challenge. So we have to believe that the future is now, this is it.

When we know that no action done in the past can bring me happiness in the present. Can neither touch me nor cause me sorrow at present. Then we are not unnecessarily worried about future karma. Worries and plans for the future will end. In such a situation, a person will never think that he will fail tomorrow. What will happen to my reputation? When we are disconnected from the past, we are disconnected from the future as well. In such a situation, my present will become the best.

The future is also an extension of the past, what we sowed yesterday. If you get happiness tomorrow, then organize it again. Organizing is not wrong but making relationships is wrong. Whether it is about liberation or getting something in life, when this feeling comes, it should be understood that the past has not been experienced yet. Whenever there is a vision of the future, it should be thought that it is a plan. Remember that now is the future and now is also the past.

Faith is cosmic, it is divine. Devotion is spiritual, it is personal. Meditation is mental and yoga is physical. We start with the body, then go to the mind, then to the soul and finally to Brahman. Rishis say that first there is faith in Brahman, then devotion in the soul, then meditation in the mind and finally yoga in the body, then every step will be easy. If you walk in reverse, every step is difficult.

Kaivalya Upanishad

Life is new every moment, if you celebrate every moment

Where life touches new directions every moment, enters through new horizons and meets new sun. There the search for newness is wrong. New Year comes every year. Every day is new. Every day we cross the darkness and step into the new dawn. We meet the new morning, every day we meet with the new wonder of life, even after that it is surprising that there is no awareness of the new in our lives. Life brings every year a new day, a new year. Pushes the old years into the pages of history every time. New Year does not come by changing the calendar.

Life has been traveling on this earth for four billion years. Every day, annually, Samvatsar and Yug and Kalpa always the search is on to find something new. Even though we don't know where we are going. A story was read. Once a horse rider was running very fast down the road towards the kutcha path. A knowledgeable person standing on the other side of the road called out to him, Sir! Where are you going so fast? The rider said that he did not know. Ask my horse, that is where he is taking us. That horse is the one who is making our life difficult. That horse is our mind. Why this story? We are not in a race to make life simple. We make every effort to make it complicated and difficult. We all are like this in life. Come fast. Where are we going?

Life is a continuous flow. Nothing remains old from waking up in the morning till sleeping at night. Trees, roads, friends, office, relationships, flowers, tables, sun everything changes a little. But there is man that wants to live in the old, lives and thinks that nothing new is happening. To experience the new, every phenomenon has to be experienced directly, be it a person, a flower, a stone or a leaf. Every moment has to be turned into a celebration to experience something new in life. Mahatma Gandhi wrote in 1932 that let's see what you decide in the New Year. Speak to the one to whom you have not spoken. Meet the one whom you haven't met. Go to whose house you haven't gone. To do all this is to welcome the new. Nothing will happen with resolution. Same resolution every year- will exercise daily. Will not eat sugar. Will focus on family. Nothing will happen from this, when the whole life can be resolved. When every moment can be turned into a celebration, the search for future resolutions and celebrations is futile.

There are two dimensions of happiness in life. One dimension is that we seek joy in every passing moment. Dedicate your energy towards the attainment of some future goal, object and keep working continuously to achieve it. In such a situation, we do not reach anywhere. They just remain as a means. We see every present as future and future as present and past and our dimension of happiness, the search for the goal itself becomes the goal and goes to the other side of the horizon. There is another dimension to the attainment of happiness – now and in the present. Instead of looking for happiness in an object or goal, find it in the present. When joy is attached to us, we are the goal itself. Everyone can find happiness in the power of consciousness, now and in this present. Don't spend your energy for the future or for achieving any of its goals. Our goal should be to simply enjoy the moment and realize it in its entirety. There are endless reasons to celebrate. There are limitless opportunities to experience bliss. Flowers are blooming, birds are singing, moon and stars have appeared in the sky. The winds are blowing slowly, the full moon with the waves is stirring our mind. We are breathing. We have dad with us yes, there are children. What little reason is this? Today to celebrate! Celebrate it all. Feel the joy

In this nature only human determines the time. Waits for the occasion – to celebrate. There is always a festival going on in nature. Everyday flowers of different colours are blooming from the same tree. New shoots are taking the place of old leaves. The festival of the sun with the moon and the stars continues daily. There is no New Year in nature. There is an experience of Diwali, Holi and novelty every day.

Only this moment is true. This is the first thing we have to understand. The realization of the new in life is a reminder of the continuous flow. Everyday everything is getting new. Tomorrow when we wake up it will be new. Everything that is old this evening will change tomorrow. But man is going on living in the old. Wants to hold on to the word yes. Instead of celebrating life, we celebrate words. We are not able to take the feeling of joy at the level of emotion. French thinker Jean-Paul Sartre named his autobiography after the word. Words and lots of words and sentences made up of them. The pronunciation. And pronounced loudly. The thought of words within the mind. We have become used to living by words. We have become used to the wording. Osho says that from birth till death we live in the world of words – thoughts, memories, fantasies and dreams are all words. The word is related to our world, our external life which has nothing to do with celebration and joy. If this was not the case then why would Alexander have kept on accumulating immense wealth for the sake of happiness throughout his life!

Life is new every moment, if there is a journey from words to beyond words. The journey of words is our outward journey. First stop on the inner journey. After which comes the level of thought and after that comes the level of philosophy. If we want to enjoy every moment of life, if we want to celebrate it, then after this third level, we have to travel to the fourth level, which is called the world of meditation. There is joy in every moment on this floor. Celebration is going on every moment on this floor. Eckhart Tolle says in his book The Powerful Present that the more we focus on the past and future of time, the more we lose sight of the present, which is the most precious thing. It has been said that tomorrow never comes. Similarly, innovation also does not happen somewhere in the future. Every moment is new.

Time is scarce in the real world and perhaps this is the reason why you spend your whole life running around trying to save time. The distinction between past, present and future is nothing but a permanent and perpetual illusion.

Albert Einstein

What is free in the world is priceless in life

What is the most valuable thing in this world? You will get the answer job, home, health, money, gems, gold etc. are precious things. But this is not true. What is free in the world is the most valuable. Sleep, air, water, peace, joy, celebration, light, fire and more breaths. The most valuable things in life and the world are those which have no value and cannot be valued. It is true but we do not see it. The reason for this is to engage the mind and intellect in thoughts. This simple truth will be revealed the day we become thoughtless. We will understand how rare things are that are simple and common.

The aspiration to be extraordinary, the desire for valuable things and the attitude of touching the pinnacle drive us crazy. But we do not know that what becomes ordinary in life, what is simple becomes extraordinary. But no one wants to be ordinary, ego does not even allow it to happen. That's why we keep on incessantly searching for insomnia, hunger, fear, anxiety, happiness. The day the truth is known, that day time runs out of our hands. There is a story that - a king built a beautiful palace, on whose main gate mathematical formulas were written. He announced that the one who solves the formula and opens the door, only then the door will open. Many scholars have come and gone. Many people united day and night in solving mathematical formulas. The door didn't open. When a seeker got time, he closed his eyes and meditated for a few moments. After this, when the door was pushed slowly, that door opened. The king asked the seeker, how did you open the door so easily? The seeker said that a voice came from within that first see whether the door is closed or not! I just followed my heart.

Life is also like this. We have already assumed that there is a problem. What is valuable has a great price. To be extraordinary is to work hard. Sometimes life tells us that there is no problem. It is our thoughts that have created such thinking. One day my younger daughter Pihu comes in front of me after buying ice cream. Eats it once. Then gives it to me. Papa! Now you eat I say - why? She said *khao na tasty hai*. I say that you have tasted and making me fool. His answer is - No. Where is the liar? I was just checking whether this ice cream is sweet or not! The matter reaches the heart.

To be extraordinary, you have to sacrifice your lust. To become valuable one has to become ordinary like tree, river, and moon, animal. One has to practice living life in simplicity and awareness like him. The temptation to accumulate is an obstacle to being extraordinary. Ego is a hindrance in the precious. The day Buddha became ordinary, made his consciousness emotionless, the same day he became precious and extraordinary. Gandhiji had gone to understand the whole of India. Went to visit India in suit-boots, and when he returned, he had only one loincloth left. He became a Mahatma the same day.

What do we want? Full of joy, fresh air, complete peace, unlimited joy, conscious breath and endless celebration. There is no need to pay any price for this. It's free. We spend our life in its search and desire. Steve Jobs wrote before his death that I am here in the dark looking at the green light of the life supporting machine. At the same time, I am also feeling God. I see death coming near. I want to say that when you have saved enough money for your last days then you should focus on your relationships, your art and your childhood dreams. The habit of always earning will make you a perverted person. He said that you can hire a driver for yourself but no matter how much money you have, you cannot hire someone for your illness. You have to bear the pain yourself.

Simplicity is our natural nature. No need to try to be simple. It just has to stop being difficult. Happiness, celebration, auspiciousness and light are not coming in our life, then the reason for this is our harshness. The heart is hard, the mind is subject to lust. Due to which the seeds do not germinate and if there is no germination then from where will joy, light or auspiciousness emerge? Our problem is that in the pursuit of the precious we forget the simplicity. We lose awareness in the pursuit of the extraordinary, and then we do not even realize that what is simple, what is aware, is also valuable. He is extraordinary and has no value, He is free.

In creation we tune into frequencies that correspond to physical reality. But in the same room there exist a myriad of parallel realities, even though we cannot tune into them.

Steven Weinberg

The sky that contains everything

Theosophical Society, a leading organization in the spiritual field, was a great saint. H. P. Blavatsky. She says in her spiritual book Sapta Dwara of Samadhi (Seven Petals of Samadhi) that the sky that surrounds us from all sides, which is also within us, is in our breath. Without which we cannot be and we were not, what was then, and what will be when we will not be. Aakash means the one who has everything. Space, the space in which all things are. Everything is created within the sky. The sky does not become smaller than that. Who has everything and who is not in anyone? The sky is not just above, it is right at our feet.

Just above the earth, where the sky begins. A space. Which is infinite. Achhor (No boundary) is there is no distinction in that, no restriction. That is flight. Buddha calls it liberation. That's why the philosophy of life is- Be huge, be the sky. Being empty, cover the horizon. Whether it is the edge of this sky or the void of Vyom (AIR) is undefined. There is infinity, its end. In this not one earth but many earths, many galaxies and many universes find their place. That's why its power is limitless. The sky is where our heaven is. Because he is on top. While looking at the sky, the form will go on disappearing. The incorporeal will become intense. The sky points us towards the formless. From where he got the lesson of divinity, he became a god. Like earth, fire, Varuna and wind, the sky was called a deity. If we look at the sky, then the corporeal will continue to fade away and we will merge into the formless.

Everything is in the sky - sky, water, fire, air and sky itself. But no one is tied, but the relationship is connected. The sky cries when it sees the earth burning. The sky becomes sad when the leaves of the trees leave their greenery and take on the yellow colour. He sobs when the snow melts. Why? Because with the touch of this snowy mountain, clouds, the sky feels its own. When the bird takes a long flight through the green trees, the sky breaks its desolation and establishes a dialogue. If there is sky, then there is sky. It has water, air.

Our heart should be as big as the sky. The sky is considered divine when there is not a single cloud. Absolutely clear and pure blue sky. When a person is close to the heart, hopes will not make a home in him. From hope, desires are born, which never end. A person is happiest when he is empty – of any kind of expectations.

What happens when we look at the sky? The head rises, and the mind is calm. Distance has many advantages in life. When we look at the sky, we see the sun, the moon, the stars, the clouds, the wind, the thunder of lightning, the speed of the meteor, the rain. Which we got without asking in this world. It makes life worthwhile. Gives a sense of expansion. As if it is said that the expansion of life is its basic meaning. New horizons should be searched daily. At the same time, it teaches the suppression of the ego. When we head down, they shrink. Thoughts get limited. The scope of the hand just shrinks while going to your home and family. The ground pulls towards itself. Due to which the house, water, air, sky all shrink. They get divided and get divided.

It has been told in Indian philosophy that the sky is the main element in the five elements. Water and earth are heavy in nature while air and fire are light. The sky element is invisible but vast. He covers everything. Everything is made of sky element only. When the elements of sky, air and fire are more in a person, then we will be as calm. Meditation and spirituality will play a central role in life. Due to the lack of sky element, we remain entangled in the world, materialism and self-interest. The more a person attains the divine light, the more the strength of the sky element will increase within him. Impurity of sky element through worship, meditation, chanting, remembrance of God, satsang, bhajan etc. is taken out and its net power can be increased.

Our soul is like the sky. And it is neither inside nor outside. The soul is omnipresent just like the sky. Inside as well as outside. All the incidents of life are happening there. Here no sign is created, but everything happens.

Similarly, there is no way to make the sky impure. We can draw lines on the body or in the water, but no line can be drawn in the soul or in the sky. To understand this soul, it is necessary that we take our consciousness beyond the mind. Then we will know that the soul is also inconsistent like the sky. Whether this body remains or not. The soul will continue to move with and without the body. How many earths are created and destroyed under the sky. So many civilizations have come and gone. No one's account is with the sky. Similarly, the soul also does not keep any account. He simply observes both the good and the bad with a witnessing attitude.

If a person speaks or acts with an evil thought, misery follows him. If a person speaks or acts with a good thought, happiness follows him. Like a shadow that never leaves him.

Mahatma Buddha

Anand (Bliss) is currently

Sariputta (A disciple of Mahatama Budha) asked his Guru that how do I find happiness? Then Buddha said to leave the search. Do one more thing. Live right here in the present. No need to search. Bliss is here, right now. We keep running, that's why happiness also keeps running. Our union is dependent on our pause. Happiness is not a thing that can be found. He is going with our birth. That is the pulse that is our nature. No need to find it. That's why we don't get it. Hold on to this moment.

Happiness depends on love. It is not possible with the intellect. Happiness requires literacy of the heart. Man's problem is man himself. He begins with himself and ends with himself. Life does not find any truth in the search for self-centred truth and insisting on keeping oneself busy in it. Arjuna's infighting at times leads him away from his vows. And again and again Shri Krishna has to show the expansion of consciousness. There was no illusion in the mind of Gopis (friend of Krishna), that is why they could see the complete truth even in the feet of Shri Krishna. If you go to find happiness, you will not find it. That is this very moment. Catch this moment now and you will get happiness. If we connect with the moment, then the limitless of bliss will be included in us.

There is a Zen story that someone asked the fakir why there is so much joy in your life. Where does this joy come from? Why is there no joy in my life? That fakir said that I am ready to be mine. You are not. Then that person asked the fakir to tell a way. That fakir took him out to the garden. He showed the different trees in the garden. Some big and some small. Some smiling, some silent. Everyone is silent, happy, blooming. No one has any complaints anywhere. Our problem is ourselves.

Every moment of life is important. And the value of any moment is no more or less than any other moment. One cannot wait for an opportunity to enjoy. Nor is the juice of joy hidden in any occasion. Happiness is in making each moment your own. A short story On the Nirvana of a Sadhu, his disciples were asked what the late Sadguru considered the most important thing in his life? He replied that the same in which he was engaged at any given moment.

Bliss is not to enjoy anything, but to associate yourself with anything. Since our attitude is such that first we want to have or possess so that we can enjoy. But bliss means to look with love. There is neither taking nor giving in this. Where there is lust, there is absence of joy. We want to get, we want to have monopoly over it. When lust dominates us, then the attainment of pleasure will be linked to the object and in love the object will also take the form of an awakened human being.

One moment is enough for joy. There is only a moment of joy. The rest is an act of uniting oneself with Him. A celebration of raindrops, a house bathed in sunlight, a delicious meal, an opportunity to travel, etc. It is a momentary event. If you get connected with him, then there is no joy or sorrow. We seek happiness throughout life because we are attached to work and the fruits of work. Celebration is going on every moment in the world. When we do something considering it as duty, we will not get happiness. Mahabharata is the best example of this. Shri Krishna calls his every deed as Leela. That's why his whole life is a celebration. Gita's preaching in the battlefield, only a leeladhari can extract the tune of the flute by stepping on the hood of Kalia Nag.

When we see people fill their lives with work, then we wish for success. Let's wait for the moment of bliss. Waiting for one happiness after another. Always worried about money, happiness, work. Have you ever seen such a man who fills life with the music of nature, the songs and dances of the Panchabhutas? Bliss or happiness, it is always momentary. When its juice is found in a moment, that moment can be eternal. Whether it is happiness or sadness, if it is long, it will only bring sorrow. That's why it is important that we be gracious. Morning sunlight is right, but evening darkness is wrong. The heat is wrong but the rain is right. This dichotomy will not do. If the morning is beautiful then beauty has to be seen in the evening as well. It is a defect of vision. We will shake hands with the man. But will hesitate to hug the tree. We do not hold a piece of stone with as much love will take it as much as any fruit. Beauty will be seen in the flower but not in the leaves. While all this is the manifestation of the same existence. If we go to the banks of rivers and seas, we will never take the trouble of sitting on the banks to pick up a grain of sand. There is a story.

Used to listen in childhood. A monk went astray while begging and reached a village in the evening. The people of that village were very strange. When the monk reached the village, he knocked on a house. This is night time. The door opened, the man asked the reason and closed the door. He said oh god you go somewhere else. We can't welcome you. My view doesn't match with your view. The monk went to many houses, but the answer remained the same. He could not find a place to live anywhere. Finally defeated, he slept under a tree outside the village at night. Due to the cold, that monk woke up in the middle of the night, then he saw that the Kalkal River was flowing near the tree, on the other side there was a panoramic view of the mountain and the forest. The sky above is full of stars, the trees are blooming with flowers. And its fragrance is captivating the atmosphere all around. Then in no time he attained silence and awareness. In the morning he ran to the same village, and knocked on a door. When that person opened the door, the monk said don't panic. I have not come to stop but to thank you. By your grace, I have known true happiness today. Felt the fragrance of Narsingk flowers. So the situation does not depend on us.

Solitude is in the mind of man. One can maintain complete peace of mind even being in the middle of the market. Such a person always lives in solitude. Another person cannot control his mind even in the jungle. He cannot be said to be in solitude. Solitude is the attitude of the mind, a man who clings to things in life cannot be in solitude, wherever he may be.

Raman Maharishi

God is the name of the feeling of divinity

Man can fly at the speed of sound and through internet he can talk to the person sitting on the other side of the world. In such a situation a question always arises in the mind that where is God? Who is it? What is? How does it look? God resides inside every consciousness. Wherever there is divinity, there is God. Dr. Parsingar established a laboratory in Canada's Laurentian University, in which he told by a subtle attack on the temporal lobe that a person has divine experience. Similarly, VS Ramachandran in the University of California has proved that there is a God spot in the human brain. We have believed in God in every particle. Shankar resides in pebbles.

What does this mean? Will he bless us by offering arghya (offering) to the sun, saluting or praying? No. Otherwise, by doing this, light will automatically enter the heart. We will be able to end the darkness.

That's why there is prayer - *Tamso Ma Jyotirgamaya*. Divinity came upon seeing the light. Feelings awakened after seeing the tree. A divinity should be transmitted in our being. That's why Hindus pray to mountains, rivers, trees, animals etc. all living and non-living things, so that life is filled with divinity. That's why the whole creation was considered a part of divinity. And an attempt was made to add coherence to it.

Socrates became a philosopher in the West. Socrates was walking on the beach when he saw a crying child. When he asked the boy the reason for crying, he said - I want to fill the ocean in this bowl in my hand but it is not happening. Socrates started crying after listening to the child. Now the child asked why are you crying. Is your bowl somewhere too? Socrates said that you want to fill the sea in a small bowl and I want to fill the knowledge of the whole world to God in this small intelligence. Today you have taught that the ocean cannot be filled in a bowl. After hearing this, the child threw the bowl into the sea and said that if the ocean cannot contain you in the bowl, but the bowl can contain the sea. After hearing this, Socrates fell at the feet of the child and said that the formula of life has come in my hands. When a person's ego disappears, then God's grace is received.

A person full of divinity has become Bhagyawan i.e. God. The fullness of such divinity leads to the experience of opulence and bliss in life. That's why it was said that the meaning of God is Sachchidananda (He is true, good and bliss). Rivers, trees, mountains, and living beings were worshipped. Where there is speed, there is progress, it was considered synonymous with divinity and it was hoped that human beings should also fill themselves with all that divinity. The meaning of God is to be full of divinity. To associate life with progress, to fill divinity and to expand opulence and to live in bliss. God is the one who does this.

Every human being at one time or the other is someone's god, even if only for a few moments. This can happen once or it can happen many times. What is God after all? God is the light of the best in man. This light is within each person. But it blossoms only when one is filled with love, compassion or compassion. The part of divinity can sometimes be small and sometimes big. Nature has always been respected in the Indian thought tradition. From mountains, rivers, sun, moon to trees and plants, reverence has been a part of our daily life. In this contemplative tradition, God is not somewhere in a temple or a temple, but he has been in front of us in the forms of various elements of nature, such as: earth, water, fire, air and sky.

God is experience, not proof. He does not come in words, nor does he get bound in arguments. No matter how many songs you sing, something is left out. Osho has written in relation to Rabindra Nath Tagore that in the last moments of life, tears were coming out of Gurudev's eyes, then his disciples asked that you should be satisfied. Life has got a destination, what is needed now? Tagore said that just now he had started feeling the song of that divine a little, was able to see the feeling of its beauty that the time has come to leave. If there is an eye then God is still there – in the waves of the wind, in the chirping of the birds, in the rays of the sun, in the leaves of the trees.

Why questions arise when incidents are happening in life. Similarly, no one has been able to know God by knowing him. Modern science came to know about the movement of blood in the body only three hundred years ago. What is God? It is like asking a fish where the ocean lies. Where is the sea our answer to that fish will be that what is all around is the ocean? Similarly this divine life has to be lost in the ocean. Just like ice starts melting in summer, in the same way, if we start getting lost in different forms and shapes in life, then we will be able to experience God. God appears in different forms but we are the ones who do not recognize him. And every day they do rituals like request, prayer, worship, pilgrimage and fasting etc. We do not see what is close to us. I don't remember what I am. What is far away is visible, calls and attracts. Moon and stars attract, Himalaya calls. The waves of the ocean are visible. But what is inside the man, his voice is not heard. The truth of life is that we live, take birth and die in God. There is God in every breath.

Sa yo ha vai tat parambrahmei brahmaiva bhavati. Nasya Brahmavit Kule Bhavit. Tarati mourning, Tarati Paanam Guhagranthibhyo. (That is, one who knows that Supreme Brahma, he becomes Brahma. No one who does not know Brahma is born in his family. He gets wet from sorrow, gets wet from sin and becomes nectar by being free from the knots of the heart.)

Mundak Upanishad

Our vision determines the future

What is life vision? How is it related to development? Drishti means to see, to contemplate. Thinking about your future or any subject. It is said in the hymns of the Rigveda that in the beginning there was only desire, which was the first seed of the mind. This drishti (i.e. vision), that is, the point of view, is the catalytic element, due to which anything takes shape. Life or development takes its course. The choice of life vision or path is not without reason. This is not possible without any inspiration. There are reasons for vision. Whether it is a matter of choice or choice. There is a reason behind the choice. And depending on this, what will be our path? The choice of options goes on throughout life. If standing at a crossroad or crossroad, will contemplate and as a result will choose a path. We have very little say in whatever choice we make. This environment, person, environment, inspiration or influence only motivates the process of our choosing. In such a situation, the importance of vision increases.

When a vision is formed, it affects the whole development. An attitude of seeing should be made keeping in mind the positive and welfare of all. Now there is conflict in the universe, so cooperation is also visible. Unity in the world, recognition of mutual complementarity between diversity and development will be good for everyone. Each one of us wants happiness, peace, love and development. Our wish is positive. But we want to reach it through negative ways. We want peace but through power and might. Want happiness but through wealth. Wants development through the destruction of others. If we want development by suppressing someone weaker than us, by corruption or by destroying nature, then that is the path of destruction. Wants love in life, but through jealousy and self-loathing. We have been made like this in the social system in which we are living today.

Positive thinking or overall life vision is the primary or rather fundamental condition of our life. It is not only concerned with a hopeful life. Its expression is through creativity in life. This creativity is possible only through the path of truth which is not mere reality of facts. Real or real cannot mean truth. Truth has to do with content. That's why truth has been a controversial word in Indian rhetoric. It has been explained time and again. The Upanishads called it Brahman, while the Buddha called it sorrow. Nature was considered truth in our philosophy, then the medieval sages considered human beings as truth. In this era of consumerism, whatever ideal life we imagine for ourselves, all its links are entangled with power and wealth. This is where the sources of all the confusions of today's life are hidden. The reason for not understanding them is that our vision is based on fragmented or negative thinking. We think in pieces.

It is not possible to solve the problem by thinking in pieces. The whole life has to be considered as a composite of the whole universe. The problem can be solved only by adopting a holistic approach. Presently, all the modern socio-political and economic ideologies are the product of western outlook, which originated mainly from two concepts. The first concept is- Man is separate from this whole creation and he has the power and right to act according to his will. The second concept is - man there is duality. The innate tendencies of the human body are in conflict with the boundless aspirations of the mind. Since the mind of the individual is different, therefore every human being is in conflict with the human being himself. After this some ideas were propounded, which became due to geographical discovery, decline of feudalism and rise of modern capitalism-imperialism. These ideas were struggle for existence, existence of almighty, exploitation of nature and individual rights and freedom. A flurry of theories were put in place to replace these ideas. The tradition of substituting these ideas, starting with Charles Darwin, went through Adam Smith's Wealth of Nations, to David Easton and other political thinkers. These thinkers said that politics is over. When politics is over, what is left? After this came ideas like end of history, end of civilization. When all the ideas to give direction to man and his life have come to an end, then where is the justification of values and ideas? This was followed in the late 20th century by the idea of privatization and privatization, in which nothing remained of the state. The society went into the background. Only the person and his conflict remained together. This duality rejected every norm and standard that would have given superiority to the human being. However, during the period of replacement of these ideas, an attempt was made to give alternatives. For the first time, Karl Marx presented the analysis of dialectical materialism through Das Kapital as an alternative to materialistic ideas.

In India, on the other hand, the struggle for existence was not considered. Here the supreme element pervades the entire universe – 'Sarvam Khalvidam Brahma' and hence harmony and co-operation prevails everywhere. The struggle we see is due to our ignorance and illusion. Similarly, the principle of existence of the best is also wrong, then what will happen to the children, old people and the weak-poor society? It was said in India – *Sarve Bhavantu Sukhinah*. The measure of any culture lies in how much it cares for its weak, crippled and marginalized society. Marx's principle of 'giving from each according to his ability' and giving to each according to his need came true in the Hindu family. Social rules should be there to protect the weak. Today families are breaking up. From the joint family came the idea of the nuclear family, which had brothers and sisters apart from the parents. Later it also got eroded. Now husband and wife have become a single family. See the squid of materialism - this single family is also disintegrating. Husband separated, wife separated.

Indian life does not support the exploitation of nature. It believes in harnessing nature. Nature has been asked to take only as much as we need. It is a bond of affinity with nature. We say- Mother Earth, Mother Cow, Mother Tulsi, Mother Ganga, Vanadevi, Kuldevi. We worship Peepal, feed milk to snakes, feed water to birds and sugar to ants. It is this worshipful attitude that prevents us from exploiting. We do not exploit that which is respected and loved. With the invention of Cresco graph, Jagdish Chandra Bose showed that plants also have a sensitive nervous system and various colourful expressions to perceive pleasure and pain. Like the animal world, the tree world also has feelings of love, hatred, joy, fear, happiness, sorrow, confusion, attachment and other innumerable types of stimuli as a reaction. Metals, trees and animals are all subject to the same general law. All of them experience fatigue and depression in basically the same way – a kind of steady, silent feeling of recovery or bliss, shivering or even death. Trees also have a circulatory system. Similar to the blood circulation in the body of animals, there is also a circulatory system in trees. Not only this, the steel used in scissors and machines etc. also experiences fatigue and on getting rest in between, its freshness and efficiency increases again. Unless this integrated feeling and philosophy will not be included in thought and action. We will give fragmentary theory. Due to this the hope of unbroken life in the society will not be fruitful.

Honesty, hard work, and considering one's own good in the good of all is the truth. This is the biggest penance, it is not in everyone's control to do or understand this, the person who can do this, he is the biggest ascetic.

Chanakya

The purpose of life is hidden in the fullness of our significance

What will be the meaning of this life? In what is the meaning of life hidden? When we are young from childhood, the feeling of making life meaningful comes in our mind. How does this meaningfulness come to perfection? The meaning of life is happiness, joy, mixture of happiness and sorrow or something else. Life means life is like roaming circle. We enter this life. We pass through its winding path. During the journey, the search for happiness, the stages of peace and the moments of respect are found and finally at some stop of this journey, rest is reached. The question comes around again. Life ie. The interval between birth and death. It's okay. But only that much. Life means happiness, peace and respect or an infinite desire for sorrow, lack and enjoyment.

The definition of life is possible. An interval, which is the period between birth and death on this earth. But what is the meaning of life? A long life getting your wish After all, life is about finding happiness. It is written in the Upanishads that what is infinite is the real happiness. There can be no happiness in whatever is limited. Infinity is the ultimate happiness and every person has this ultimate happiness. Try to understand B. There are many types of happiness and pleasure. Physical pleasure. Full of luxury Ego based happiness. Event based happiness. Future based happiness.

Happiness or happiness is related to the mind and the mind is fickle. Means happiness and sorrow come in the realm of fickleness. He simply enjoys it. That moment it makes that mind happy or sad. Nothing else. That is, the meaning of life is not hidden in happiness or sorrow, but in experiencing it. What do we enjoy Joy after constant trouble. Success after many failures. Showers of rain amidst the scorching heat. A smile of a child, a touch of a wife in a moment of trouble or food from mother's hand, sitting near God and finding oneself. These are some incidents. It is a matter of few moments. But it is possible that small moments like these can give meaning to life. There is no need to starve of endless happiness for this. The happiness that has no end may seem like sorrow. After all, one who is always used to delicious food, how he would understand the meaning of delicious food. Only a hungry person can know this. The meaning of life is not in eternity or immortality. It is better to dedicate one's infinite energy to Dharma like Ghatotkacha than to be immortal Ashwathama with a painful body. The meaning of life lies in immortality. So that immortality should be of Hanuman. Those who are ready to present themselves for the society every moment. Hanuman, who used to lift the huge Dronachal mountain containing sanjeevani herb, is also suffering, but for the sake of philanthropy. His Dronachal is full of medicines that give meaning to life.

As soon as we ask the question that there is something else in our life? What after this? How now? In the same way we go on a mechanism. Accepting or following any one value system is not a sign of superiority. If life is great, then it is not necessary to be mechanical or infinite. That life is the best, whose living paves the way for the waves of humanity. Give love to someone Show the way the best life or the meaning of life is not given to any king or a person sitting on a high position, but to some Meera, Socrates and Bhagat Singh. The meaning of life can also rest on our criteria. But there is no meaning of such meaning, which is not exemplary.

The one who does not bow down to see or know. There is so much in this infinite universe to love. There are many things with which to integrate. There is some significance in that. The biggest truth of life is life itself. Life is the biggest truth of the earth. But there is the ultimate truth, the realization of emptiness which is found while battling with the complexities of life. Everyone has to struggle. The goal of life is to fight and overcome complications. The whole universe is in motion. Solar systems, galaxies, the Sun and the stars are all in constant motion. As our planet grapples with ever-changing and complex times, we too must have the courage to move forward. Life has meaning only for those who move forward with faith in God and determination to conquer life's difficulties with their faith. The meaning of life is not in stagnation. This life is dynamic, so how can meaning be stable? The meaning of life is to live every moment of life to the fullest.

He wants to get whatever he desires in this world. But that is not life. The whole of mankind is troubled by the desire to get what they want. There are as many meanings and as many aspirations in this diverse life as there are people. Every man wants to find such new directions in line with his instincts where he can see the meaning of life. Life keeps changing every day. Keeps on increasing. New pages keep getting added to it. There is always a meaning with this past time, which is useful for the present. To leave the mark of our mind, consciousness and existence on the pages of the past is the goal of life, and also the meaning of life. What else besides this?

The question of meaning and futility of life has been discussed in every civilization. In every literature of the world, there is a description of such characters, who suffer the torture of life. Let's search for happiness. The description of three such characters comes in Greek literature, which was described by Dharmaveer Bharati in his poem Pramatyu-gatha. In these characters, someone's life's tortures are due to their infatuation, while someone happily suffers punishment for philanthropy. Atlas was punished for disloyalty to Devraj Zeus i.e. Indian Indra, and he is living eternal life carrying the sky on his shoulders.

And it will go on. He had a brother Prometheus. He had also committed a crime, but in public interest. He enriched mankind with Devopam Shakti, stole fire from heaven and made it available to mankind. King Pluto punished for this punishment. He was tied with an iron chain. An eagle used to eat the flesh of his stomach every day during the day, at night the wound would heal, then again the eagle would be present to eat the flesh. Prometheus continued to suffer the punishment of providing fire to mankind for thirty thousand years. Then Devraj gave him freedom.

A third character in Greek literature is Sisyphus, a resident of Aeolus. His father had the right over Vayu as a boon from Devraj. With this, he would bring weather on the earth as per his wish. One day he also died. Sisyphus got distracted, thought - Death is the most powerful. What did he think about the meaning of Prometheus' fire and joy in life? If death comes He took a vow that he would conquer death. A similar situation had come in the life of Mahatma Budha. The reason for his Mahabhinishkraman (renunciation from life) from this life was also sorrow and death in life. But he devoted his life to penance. To know the meaning of life, do sadhna for seven years in this way. It is believed that his cognition-discretion and compassion friendship reached the climax. Then he got enlightenment. He used to meditate in the form of Gautama, came in front of the world as a Buddha. With a knowledge. Interview of the Four Noble Truths. Not of sorrow, not of death. By conquering the fear of death and solving sorrows, he found the way to live life. But if Sisyphus had thought like this, he too would have become a Buddha. But he thought, when death plays tricks in our lives, then death should also be won by tricks. So when death came to take him, he was taken prisoner. Result. The person became a little dilapidated after a time, stopped walking, eating and drinking, but death did not come. Trees don't dry, flowers don't fall! New trees and flowers and fruits stopped coming. There was an outcry in nature. People had realized the tragedy of immortality and eternal life. People everywhere raised their hands demanding death. Death, death! People realized the necessity and inevitability of death. Retired after a meaningful and successful life. Of death again started a new life full of power. Death after the completion of life is better than the torment of eternal life. By the order of Devraj Zeus, Aetius showed might and defeated Sisyphus and put him in prison. King Pluto punished. Sisyphus will push the huge marble rock lying at the bottom of the Hades valley to the top of Giri-Sringa. After that the rock will be thrown down again. And Sisyphus will continue to work his way to the top. Sisyphus spent thirty-two thousand years doing this. The culprit of bringing immortality to earth is doomed to suffer meaningless punishment even after being immortal himself. After suffering the torture, he became a stone. Probably like Ashwathama. Sisyphus also failed in his attempt to overturn the natural order, and so did Ashwathama. And both are helpless to suffer the cursed life. The rock of Sisyphus is grassless, so the life of human beings on this earth is turning green by the teachings of Mahatma Buddha who conquered the fear of death.

The idea is that life is the best art of living, live a meaningful life. Live for others as well as yourself. The meaning of life does not lie in immortality and eternity. If there is life, then there is torture, there is sorrow and it has to be suffered. Now the question is how do we bear that sorrow? Bear the sorrows, face the difficulties by making the self-consciousness loving and compassionate. By bringing the warmth of love in the coldness of life. This is the meaning of life. That's why it was said in Indian thinking, *muhurtam jwalitam shreyah, na cha chiram dhumayait*. It is better to glow with the radiance of the moment, than to stare for a long time. The biggest truth of life is life itself.

Na yatha yatne nityam yadbhavayati tanmayah. Yadgichechch Bhavitum Tadbhavit Nanyatha. i.e.That is, man tries as usual. As he feels and as he wants to be, he becomes like that, otherwise not.

Yoga Vashishtha

The infinite journey of life begins with self-awakening

The sages pray – *Om Asto Ma Sadayagamaya, Tamaso Ma Jyotirgamaya Mrityo Ma Amritogamay.* O Supreme Father, let us go from untruth to truth, from darkness to light and from death to immortality. How do we get this truth? How to spread the light of knowledge in our lives? And how can we be free from the fear of death. These things have been explained beautifully and elaborately in

Vrihadaranyakopanishad. The writers of the Upanishads say that it depends on the vision. If our vision changes, the perspective of seeing the universe changes. The author of the Upanishads wrote after self-interview that when the Self initially saw itself, it felt that only I am here. There is no one else. That's why there is no reason to fear. The sages give the message that fear, arrogance, anger, hatred are generated only by accepting the presence of someone other than oneself. Not only this, when we accept our existence too rigidly, ego arises, which is the reason for bondage. At the time of the origin of the universe, that self-element was later considered synonymous with Brahmatva. And later that Supreme Being created various creatures and elements in the universe with its determination power.

Determination power is the biggest thing. This is the essence of this Upanishad. A meeting of all the Brahmavetas was called in the Rajya Sabha of King Janak. It was to be decided that who is the best Brahmagya? It was decided to give them thousand cows. The philosopher Yajnavalkya, present in the assembly, asked his disciple Soumya Samashrava to take these cows to our hermitage. After this, debate started between Yajnavalkya and all the philosophers present in Brahmasabha. Yajnavalkya defeated the group of nine best philosophers of that time with his logic, philosophy and enlightenment. Among the Upanishads, the oldest and the largest in size is the Upanishad Vrihadaranyaka. Philosopher Yajnavalkya is the author of this Upanishad. This Upanishad is a branch of Shukla Yajurveda which means Vrihat i.e. big and Aranyaka i.e. forest. Yajnavalkya proved the supremacy of his knowledge by discussing scriptures with all the great philosophers of the time in the court of King Janak. Had discussions with learned women like Gargi, Maitreyi and Katyayani and philosophers like King Janaka, Udalaaka Aruni, Vidagadha Shakalya, Jaratkarava Artabhaga, Ushasta Chakrayana, Kohal Koshitkeya.

After debate, the creator of the Upanishad said that there was nothing in the beginning of the universe except the Self. When that soul looked around itself, it could not see anything except itself. This instilled in him the feeling that the ego exists, that is, I am the only one. Because of this ego, all the confusion, all the troubles and fears have arisen. Sages pray to avoid this O Lord, lead me from untruth to truth. This call is extraordinary because man naturally falls down. Our desire, our deeds and our lust always lead us towards Asad. Because of this desire, this action, our lust, even if we do nothing, we will go down, because in the search of happiness and ease, the soul forces us to go down a little. The call from below is ever resounding, and Nature cooperates in it with all her instruments. If lust prevails, if desire is paramount, then man would prefer to turn to stone. Consciousness itself is the cause of suffering. Socrates has a cup of poison in his hand. His co-workers ask that you are not afraid of death? We have planned to free you from this prison. Socrates says that I am already free. What kind of fear what kind of jail the person who knows the Self is not afraid of sorrow? We are afraid of suffering. Queen Kunti prays to Shri Krishna that Vipad Santu Ta: Shashwattatra Tatra Jagadguru. Bhavato darshanam yatsyadapunarbhavdarshanam. Give us pain I want sorrow because on this pretext I should keep remembering you. May no happiness or frenzy of ego arise in my mind? This lust for happiness, this sense of ego keeps on pulling us down.

And when a man reaches a helpless state, then he has to pray that O Lord, lead me towards the right path, towards the light. This prayer is requested to our soul, the soul sitting inside. When this feeling gradually becomes dense, then our aspiration starts guiding our actions. Eddington was a great scientist who received a Nobel Prize, he wrote in his memoirs that now at the end of life the truth is being revealed that the world is not a group of things. This universe resembles more a thought than a thing. Mahatma Buddha said the same thing in his first sermon of Dhammapada that what you think, you will become. That's why think about something with honesty and thought. Our good feelings or bad feelings get concentrated and become our conduct. Prayer is a medium to make our consciousness move in an upward direction. Through this the person surrenders completely. There is no other medium in life where dedication is complete. When the surrender is complete, then only the journey of truth will begin. Otherwise this soul will always be busy with lust, pleasure and ego.

May every breath, every step be filled with immense peace, joy and purity. We just need to be awake, alive in the present moment.

thich nyat han

Victory over despair is possible only with a calm mind

Once the Dalai Lama was asked in a press conference that it doesn't bother you to think what the Chinese did to you and your people? The Buddhist religious leader said that the Chinese have taken everything from us, but will not let them take my mental state. No matter how big the situation of hopelessness may be in life, there may be a whirlpool of despair, but it is always necessary to keep the mind calm and healthy. That is what the most effective means is. If someone gets possession of it, then there is no option left. If the mind is calm then there is no dearth of options and possibilities in life. Those who hammered nails into Mahavir's ears were also found. He was stoned. They were chased away during discourses in the village, but Mahavir always used to say that *Vair Majjh na Kewai*. That means I have no enmity with anyone. If it is his, then only he knows.

There is a Zen legend that Bokuju went to his master. His teacher told that look Bokoju, now a difficult phase of meditation is coming. Do not be afraid when the state of Buddhahood comes. Don't even have any attachment. Stay away from both attachment and detachment. If any situation comes, then cut it with the sword. Bokoju asked Gurudev, but from where will I get the sword in Sadhana? Then the Guru said that from where wisdom will come in meditation, the sword will also come from there. Mind is the cause of all tendencies. If someone speaks with a guilty mind. Karma does. So misery follows him like a bull pulling the wheel of a cart and his feet. To get out of depression. If you want to end despair, you have to meditate on the mind.

Why is it necessary to keep calm in despair? The simple answer is that any instinct first arises in the mind. We go through the way. Looks like a beautiful building. There is no desire to see the building. Nor is it wrong. But there is no neutral feeling that saw and left. When the shadow of that building overshadows the state of mind, then there is a problem. Mind is a sound. The mind creates a scene, if the sound is organized then it is okay. There is nothing wrong if the picture comes and goes on the camera of the mind. But the mind becomes chaotic. When you start listening to that sound, start running after the picture, then there is a problem. That's why Buddhist gurus say that it doesn't matter if everything is taken away from a man, but the mind should remain calm and healthy.

Life depends on the use of opportunity. Success comes only when possibilities are converted into creation. Just keep your eyes open, and be on the lookout for the smallest opportunities. This is also necessary because whenever a crisis situation comes before us, we are left with no options. That's why one should be prepared for any situation at all times. Analysing this civilization, Steven Pinker says that the incidents of violence and murder have decreased continuously in the world passing century after century. But the reality is not like this. There is not much we can do to overcome the fear or depression prevailing in the society and the world. Our despair, depression and fear one reason for this is our greedy attitude. Our expectations are increasing more and more. In the world we live in, we are taught what is wrong with being greedy and having expectations. We have to understand that greed has not brought any improvement in the situation of poverty and hunger in the world.

The cause of our despair is more pleasure, more greed, more money, and the desire for more. If we are conscious then our aim should be that every living being in the world should be free from suffering, everyone should get happiness and peace. Shouldn't this be our aim? The people of the present generation are fast turning away from the idea and it is being replaced by the darkness and violence of cruelty. The absence of a worthy role model has filled our lives with anger and depression. Instead of showing our excellence and innovation, we are insisting on copying. If we want to be effective in life then we must have a calm and stable mind. Being angry or discouraged due to frustration may be our natural expression, but if we nurture anger or stay stuck in anger, it makes us normal.

Everything in creation is within you. Ask everything from yourself.

Rumi

The sweetness of life lies in flowing like a river

Listen to the river saying that there is neither fear of falling from the peak nor does it care about the flow hitting the rocks. There is neither the fear of his crying and the bondage of the edges, nor the temptation to stop and settle his family. And yes! Who saw the sea? There is speed, there is rhythm and together it sings and waves its moment. That's just life. The form and action of the river itself has a glimpse of the philosophy of creation and life. The person who becomes like the water of the river, becomes successful. Liquid like water, simple and graceful, for him even an obstacle becomes an opportunity. River means the infinite form of water drop by drop. A trip. Of civilization, of tradition, of celebration of life, of creativity.

The journey of the ocean from the formation of a drop. Many water streams coming out of the origin of mountains and mountains together form a river. After jumping in the hilly paths, it spreads its fertility in the field, taking the form of a huge river by meeting many rivers like itself. The fluidity of the river means becoming humble. If it is simple, then flowing like water, you will reach your destination! The river does not flow anywhere, that is why it does not stop. If these rivers were not there, then our great Indus-Aryan civilization would not have happened. Its continuous movement has been the energy and strength of the eternal journey of Indian civilization. Build cities on the banks of the river, shrines at the confluence, fertile and cultivable land at the ends and shelter for countless creatures at the bottom. If Sun is a living deity, then rivers are the medium to know existence. It gave occasion for celebration by giving happiness in human life. With her finesse, she created the basis of spirituality and poetry with ease. River and human have only one melody in life. Just as rivers coming out of mountains and forests merge into the ocean touching countless stones, fields, trees and life, in the same way human beings merge innumerable feelings, sorrows, learning and joy in the journey of life and merge into the ultimate. Shri Krishna is an example of this. Started life on the banks of a river and ended his pastimes on the banks of the sea. Maybe that's why I can never forget RC Prasad Singh's poem- what is this life It is waterless, its water is fun. Running on both the arrows of happiness and sorrow is arbitrariness.

A lesson of persistence can be learned from the river. In addition to consistency, river listening can be learned. To listen with a steady heart, with a waiting, generous soul, without agitation, without desire, without passing judgment, without expressing opinion. The river has many voices. There are notes of life in it, there are notes of continuity of existence. There are many forms. Water evaporates, rains, forming fountains, streams and rivers. In the same way, a living river always flows in this body of our life, which passes through the spinal cord. The flow of energy in the spinal cord continues to flow from the Sahasrara of the brain to the Muladhara. Just as the rivers of our social life have become polluted, similarly the flow of the river inside the body has also not remained clean. We have polluted the inner river with the garbage of our anger, hatred, fear, violence and greed. The cleanliness of this inner river is also necessary for the upward ascent of man. For this energy has to be taken from the bottom up.

How many secrets does the river have? Its water is constantly flowing, flowing and flowing, yet it is always there. Yet every moment is new. It is the river which is everywhere at the same time. At the source and the mouth, at the spring and ghat, in the stream, in the ocean and on the mountains. The existence of everywhere and the present is only for Him. Neither for the shadow of the past, nor for the shadow of the future? In life too, there is neither past nor future. There is no such thing, which will always remain in its original form, but there is reality in everything. Who can understand this? The river teaches to listen. It teaches that to go deep into life is to discover life. Everything is acceptable to the river. He has to be there. This is love. We all always have a simple and pure mind, like a river. He never gets old, always remains innovative. There is never any dirt in the mountain river. She washes away all the filth of the past moments. Then a mind as clear as glass. Not even a speck of memory remains. There is no fear of future in his mind.

The pain of the river is unique. It gives the message that when we are in natural love then only we can love with human being. , When the mind becomes like a river, then only that mind listens, waits... being happy. The love of the river is everlasting. His magic is strange. He gives love to our society, fills us with devotion, but what do we give in return? But no one can hurt these rivers. She is flowing. Always, forever.

Silence is a great teacher and you must pay attention to it to learn its lessons. There is no substitute for the creative inspiration, wisdom, and stillness that come from knowing how to approach the original source of inner silence.

Deepak Chopra

Development of the society

Individual and society both are dependent on each other. Individual is a part of the society. If a person does not think about the welfare of the society, then the person will also not benefit from it. If there is no development of the individual then there will be no development of the society. Society is formed by the individual. The fabric of both is embedded in each other. The family (village or town) has a central role among the institutions that hold society together. Since the individual is at the centre of the family. Therefore, the process of social change goes along with the changes in the individual and the family. An individual's place is important in building a society. But if the society is looking for change, or is happening, then it starts at the level of the individual. The unit of the family is the individual. Therefore, a person or a society can be built or changed by making the family the base. If the person changes, the family will change. If the family changes, then the society i.e. the village and the city will change. It has been the identity and basis of Indian identity.

The one thing that held India together for centuries was its strong social structure. The role of society has always been strong in Indian life. Even at that time when the whole of India was tied in one thread. Society and family were given more importance than the individual. Even in a unitary and centralized governance system, the village and family functioned as an independent unit to strengthen and give direction to the society. However, caste, religion and wealth also played a role in this. But the society was always awake, that's why whether it is monarchy or democracy, it could never dominate the society. This society gave direction to the polity in the time of crisis. Monarchy has always been society based. Perhaps because of this also the monarchy was not as strong as it should be. Like other countries of the world, there was absence of autocratic and authoritarian rule in Indian history. Indian society has never allowed the monarchy to become so powerful. This is the reason why political power also stayed away from the life of common people in the 20th century. However, through the constitution, we strongly talked about social welfare. There was pressure from the society that democracy was adopted in India after independence. India's pluralistic society could not allow its government to become authoritarian, as happened in third world countries. Perhaps for this reason, economists like Gunnar Myrdal called India a weak state in the 60s. He had no idea of the power of Indian society. Jawaharlal

Nehru knew the power of Indian society. In his famous book Discovery of India, he defined Indian society in three words – village, caste and family.

There are more than five lakh autonomous, self-sufficient villages in the Indian society. More than two thousand castes and lakhs of families. These families used to be joint, which are now breaking up.

The idea of the Indian psyche is that society is more important than the individual. If society is important then naturally the place of family and village is paramount. The society is also built basically from these only. But now Indian society is changing rapidly. Power is being transferred from traditional society to civil society. Villages or clans had no right over the land. The state declares its authority on it. In Indian life, the society used to determine the powers, rules and regulations of the king or ruler, but now this is not the case. For a successful and strong nation, it is necessary to have effective polity and strong and awakened social structures. In a weak monarchy, there is a lack of justice-loving rule and it is not possible to stop corruption, adultery, injustice from such a ruler. Today India is moving towards a market based future. Here the role of the monarchy is limited. In such a situation, the role of the society increases a lot. When government starts projects for development, for example: irrigation, electricity, roads or any factory based, then it has to face resistance from the society. Sometimes force has to be used, but except for a few exceptions, the government has to back down. Till the completion of any development plans, the government has to face many types of resistance. In India, the decision-making capacity of governments in development plans gets paralyzed, while in other countries, projects start and end. Lack of transparency of rules and strong implementation system is one of the reasons for the failure of projects in India. Society's opposition is also the main reason.

Now the question is that when the power of the society is more than that of the government, then the society will have to develop a holistic approach towards development. Society will also have to decide the direction of development and the means of implementation. How is this possible? Naturally and definitely by empowering the village and the family. It is possible if a person develops as a unit, does not remain ideologically divided and remains devoted to the nation. For this the family has to be empowered. If the family is strong then the nation will also be successful.

On society at the level of right knowledge Transformation means cultural upgradation of man. Only a cultured man dreams of social change and builds a new society according to his ideal inspirations. This is a level of excellence. But even if social change is to increase materialism and to sacrifice human being on the altar of sensualist, then only the family and the individual are made the target. Therefore, the nation can be awakened only by empowering the individual and the society, and by making it weak, it can be made the guardian of materialistic culture.

Be at the centre of your being, because the farther you are from the centre, the less you learn. Search your heart – your way of acting becomes your being.

Lao Tzu

The measure of a person's rights

Emphasis was laid on cooperation and gradual development in Indian thought. In this regard, the thinkers said that man and nature are all complementary. The seed, the sprout, the tree's trunk, branch, leaf, flower and fruit, though distinct in appearance, are visible in the course of evolution. This visible form of the different stages of gradual development is visible to us in different forms. It would be a mistake to believe that there is a conflict between the seed and the sprout, a conflict between the stem and the branch. Someone's jurisdiction is bigger. It is a gradual development. In the same way, the different components from the individual to the entire universe also have different stages of development, and the way and to the extent that this development of the consciousness of each person has taken place, it should be considered as his right.

The more a person's consciousness, his sense of oneness has developed, the more he will have rights. This should be the yardstick of authority in modern times. Apart from being oneness with oneself, a person can also maintain such oneness with all other persons, family, society, nation, humanity, the entire universe and the universe. Integration with a higher or lower component does not reduce or eliminate the integration with other components. Yoganandji says that without inner satisfaction, even heaven on earth can turn into hell. Keeping busy in keeping and saving material things is not the goal of life. control your life. Make it as simple as you can. If we see lack of happiness or success in most people, it does not mean that this is the destiny of life. What you achieve in your gap determines your success. If there is nothing within you, you cannot have any happiness.

Globalization is the main reason behind the desire for materialistic happiness that is increasing like a mirage or Bhasmasur. The world is not accepting its good things, but we are fast moving towards those things which disturb the balance of the earth and the ecosystem. The biggest challenge of this globalization is the unrelenting flood of consumerism, hunger and cravings. Similarly, every person will get work and respect only when balance is maintained in both. It is happening today that the more financially prosperous or politically on top, he gets more prestige. This increases dissatisfaction and inequality. At present, the value of life is material and every person is troubled and longing for material prosperity, material gain and material convenience, as if it is a sign of respect and prestige. Social respect and material facilities did not go together in Indian thinking. It was said here that if the area or stature of social prestige increases, then physical happiness will decrease and if physical happiness is desired then social prestige will be less.

In this age we live in a house and every house we live in has many walls. We have to build houses where there are no walls. Perhaps that's why Kabir had said - Avadhu! The sky is home. Our inner house has to be shown the infinite and vast sky. Only then will an alternative emerge. If life is to be lived, then first the mind has to be organized. The search for peace and the search for happiness is possible not from the outside inwards but from the inside out. Something is scattered in the courtyard of the mind, if there are moments of happiness, then it has to be collected. Accept your circumstances and people as they are. Because in trying to change others, you destroy your own energy. Change yourself first, everything else will change automatically. If you feel that you are getting sorrow from someone, then give lots of blessings to such person. This will open the flow of stopped energy within you, the consciousness will be pure.

In the present environment, any system can give an alternative only as long as the essence of universality is contained in it, and due respect is given to the nature and importance of all inert, conscious and living beings. The first condition of this universal humanism will be the creation of an enlightened human being. The first responsibility of a spiritual state would be the spiritual awakening of the individual. Man himself should recognize his significance in this world. He should know that we are essentially spiritual beings who sometimes go through human experiences. In such a situation, not only do we have to identify our superiority and spirituality, but we also have to awaken that eternal consciousness within us. He wants to be awakened, so that one thinks of the individual as a whole separate from body, mind and intellect. The human body is a person and each of its subtle parts called koshas is a part. Similarly, the aggregate of all persons is God, although He himself is also a person. The universe is God. Vyashti means part and parcel of the soul. God is not a distant being, but R is the set of a being. That's why the awakening of a person is the awakening of God. After this, the second task of the spiritual state is to identify the extraordinary abilities of the individual. Everyone is full of extraordinary abilities. This quality and power is not in any other creature. When a person is determined to express himself, then he can do anything and anything can happen. After this spiritual awakening, when a person discovers his extraordinary ability, then he becomes full of humanism due to his basic nature i.e. experiences universality.

Here is a world within us – of thought, of feeling, of power, of light, of beauty. Despite being invisible, the powers of this world are most powerful.

Charles Hannell

Beauty begins in the morning and ends in the evening

What is the beauty of Surdas who was blind from birth? However, but beauty is seen in his creations. No poet with an eye has been able to do the same till date as he has mentioned the adornment of Shri Krishna from child form to youth and other forms. Therefore it has to be accepted that there is a third eye in our body, which sees, understands and expresses beauty in its expressions. Why dusk beauty? The beauty of the morning is still raw, be it of a flower, of a man. Beauty ripens in the evening. There is redness in it. Anyway every creation is born out of darkness. All beauty is related to the darkness of the womb. For this reason beauty reaches its peak in the evening.

Someone asked Osho that what is the secret of the beauty of Mahatma Buddha? His answer was that they are beautiful because they are true to being or not being themselves. His attention and love is reflected in his appearance. Beauty itself is a flower blooming on nature. The beauty of Mahatma Buddha is the result of his meditation, spiritual practice and realization of truth. A Zen story. Rionen, a Zen practitioner, was born in Japan in 1797. She was the granddaughter of the famous Japanese warrior Shingen. Her beauty was unique. For this reason she became the servant of the empress. One day the empress passed away. Then Rion decided to become a Zen practitioner. But the family did not allow. Got permission to become a Sadhika with the condition of marriage and birth of three children. He fulfilled the condition and got his head shaved and set out on the journey. She reached the city of Edo and sought permission from Zen master Tetsugaya to make her a disciple. After watching for a few moments, the Guru did not give permission, because her beauty was unique. Then she reached to Zen master Hakuo. There also the request to make disciples was rejected. After this Rionen heated an iron and put it on his face. After becoming a squid, the Zen master Hakuo accepted to make him a disciple.

She wrote a poem - When I was in the service of the empress, I used to burn frankincense. To perfume your beautiful clothes. Now I burn my face as an Aniket Sannyasin. So that I can enter, in a Zen ashram!

Beauty is never of the body. He doesn't get attached to anything. Mahatma Buddha says that beauty is only of consciousness. In that in which consciousness has expanded, beauty manifests itself in its fullness. This body is only a place of lust. This is the house of excrement. Tathagata describes 32 types of ugliness. In this, everything from hair, follicles, nails, teeth, to sweat, fat to saliva has been described. It is also correct. Foul smell comes from the body, things rot. But the foul smell does not enter the consciousness. The body becomes ugly. Things may become clumsy, but consciousness never withers. That's why the most beautiful inside the body always comes in the evening. Eternal beauty is glimpsed only after the journey of meditation on the path of life. It has a lasting fragrance. Any beauty before that is temporary. When we become aware of the power that attracts all the creations of this world towards itself and gives them stability, then only beauty is seen in all things and places.

If beauty resides in the eyes, if the ability to enjoy the moment comes, then old age is more beautiful than childhood. The beauty of the evening is thick. If we fill ourselves with the fragrance of flowers throughout the day, if we immerse ourselves in the waves of nature, a miracle will happen. Even when the flowers wither or the nature becomes calm in the evening, the fragrance and tone will be so heavy on our consciousness that the evening will seem beautiful. Sanjh has a different dignity. When the flowers wither in the evening, when the leaves fall and the birds return to their homes, they have a satisfaction. Evening will come, but if we do not embrace the celebration of nature before that, then we will be missed. Everything will wither in the evening. Morning is the beginning of beauty and evening is the climax of that beauty. Whether it is a raw person or an object, it has less eligibility. The capacity to tolerate is also not enough. When they ripen, only then they become capable of receiving even rain water. Otherwise, if it remains raw, there is a fear of melting with water. There is no lasting beauty anywhere. The flower is beautiful but will wither with the sun. Petals will fall. If the plant is small then there is a dawn of beauty in it. Evening is created by adding moment by moment. There is an expansion of consciousness in the evening. There are many colors of existence in him. Life has many dimensions. There is a grace in that. It is a connection for life. There is a longing that never fades away. As if by accepting drop by drop it becomes a lake.

Man passes through sorrow throughout his life, searching for happiness. That's why when evening comes for him, he looks like form, looks like a burden. Just carries, because there is no solution. What is the sum of our whole life, comes in the form of a burden. Rabindranath Tagore has said beautiful things that just as pure snow accumulates on the peaks of the mountains, snow peaks on the Himalayas, similarly when a person grows old after really imbibing all the joys of life, his grey hair also the beauty of a lifetime appears like a snow peak.

Man gets old, animals get old, and they don't get ugly. Their old age has the same beauty as an old tree. Even if an old tree becomes thousand years old, there is no decrease in its beauty. Her beauty increases. People sit under his shadow. Be it an old tree or an old person, it becomes the centre of meeting in villages. The fun of sitting there is something else. You don't get any experience from a young tree. When a tree becomes old, simplicity comes in it. One becomes huge after tolerating so much rain, so much cold and heat. Meeting with the moon for years, a sweet deal was done. Feeling warm with the sun. Got the feeling of walking on the path of action in the sunshine of life. Osho says that sitting near an old tree is like sitting near history. A very deep tradition flows from it. Old trees are beautiful because they are dense and large. There is beauty in an old man too. He does not have the impatience of youth. They don't rush anymore.

The beauty of dusk is eternal. Efforts are always on to save the tree under which Mahatma Buddha attained enlightenment. Not only this, Bodhi tree has been made from the branch of that tree in many countries. Preservation of the twilight of the tree is essential for the realization of that ultimate event, the witnessing of that festival and the realization of that ultimate vibration. If we sit quietly near the Bodhi tree, we experience an indescribable bliss. There is immense peace under that tree. She makes us partners in her experience.

A beautiful story on beauty. Chang Ching was a great poet. He was a connoisseur of beauty. It is said that there was no philosopher of beauty greater than him in China. She wrote wonderful and valuable books on beauty. For twenty years he was engrossed in writing the book. Kept searching for what is beauty. One day in the middle of the night, when I raised my head from the books, I could see the sky and the moon far away across the door. The tall trees looked as if they were meditating. Light wind was blowing. With those winds, the smell of flowers came up to the nose.

At the same time a bird's voice echoed somewhere nearby. Chang Ching started asking himself how mistaken I was! Raise the screen and see the world. For twenty years he could not find beauty in books. The curtain was removed and the beauty was standing in front of, in the flesh. The senses are the medium of perception. The body is its door. Our eyes, ears, nose and mouth are only windows. He who is able to see. Sees beauty in everything.

When I look at the Solar System, I see that the Earth is just the right distance from the Sun to receive the proper amount of heat and light. it can't be a coincidence

Isaac Newton

Divinity in simplicity

In the last moment of Maharishi Raman, his disciples asked that now the body is leaving. Where will you go Maharishi said where will I go. There is nowhere to go. I will remain who I am and I will remain where I am. There is only one existence and no other existence. The problem is that we are not conscious, we remain complex. It is a matter of simplicity. If it is simple, listening to the chirping of birds can be meditation. Getting absorbed in your inner voices can become a tomb. We are asleep, and life goes on dancing. We just go on searching, we don't know. While mind, emotion and body are part of this nature which is flowing in the wave of the same flow. It is very difficult to remain simple. Man oscillates between the oscillator of simplicity and complexity.

Whoever makes his mind pure like a mirror in life, then the form of God starts reflecting in him? Even if a simple person stands near a tree, he will feel the beauty of God in it. He will relish the voice of that formless in the songs of the birds. One will perceive the fragrance of God in the blooming flower. Seeing the beauty of the moon is possible only by making yourself pure and calm like a lake. How will this happen? Simplicity is the only formula. The more the human civilization developed, the more complex, harsher and more severe it has become. Simplicity has disappeared from our routine.

All the arrangement of our life is outside, while life is inside us. We are not worried about the life created inside. The truth is that our life is just a system of livelihood. We make arrangements for life outside. The bread is outside, the eater is inside. The bed is outside, the sleeper is inside. Parents, wife, children, friends are all outside. Love, compassion, friendship, relationship maker is outside. Only the spontaneity, simplicity and humility of life will be able to take us inside life. Seriousness, rigidity and complexity have no business in life. The flower is not rigid, the tree is not rigid. Air is not complicated. Water is simple, liquid. All over the world, people have made themselves heavy. The world is engaged in dance, existence is absorbed in melodious music and the world is immersed in bliss. There is juice all around. Except the man. The 19th-century European sage John Ruskin writes in his book Cooke and Wedderburn (Modern Painter, Part Five, 1860) that wherever I travel, there the man I see wherever a man goes, he destroys all the beauty of nature.

There are two types of people in life. One complex and the other simple. There are complex, who are pursuing the goal. A goal that moves a little further away every morning. Or always visible at the same distance like a mirage. The second is the simple life, in which there is no goal. Every moment is a celebration. Karma happens. There is humility towards existence, because there is an infinite reason in this universe to celebrate. Flowers are in bloom. Sun, moon and stars are visible in the sky. The birds are singing. Rivers are flowing. We are alive Are breathing. Our consciousness is getting united with all these elements.

Have you ever wondered why childhood is blissful? Why life wants to get childhood again and again. Childhood days are the days of simplicity. The heart is simple. Childhood is considered innocent, that's why joy is seen all around. As the age increases, the heart becomes hard. Then the joy also ends. If there is sorrow in life, if there is trouble, if it becomes difficult to spend time, then it should be understood that our path is complicated. Our existence in this vastness is not of equal value to that of an ant. There is no point in me being. So there is no point in making yourself complicated and difficult.

Unless a man becomes comfortable within and outside himself, it will not be possible to experience divinity in his life. Happiness will be available only in spontaneity. Where there is complexity, there will be unhappiness. Man himself is complicated. Everything is easy in this universe except man. Trees grow continuously, rivers flow. The moon and stars are rotating on their axis. There is no complexity in this huge event. Everything is getting easier. There is no explosion anywhere. Lao Tzu believes that humanity or simplicity is of the nature of water. They say that there is nothing gentler and devoted than water, yet there is nothing that equals it in attacking the hardest of things. Surrender overcomes the harsh and the soft overcomes the harsh, but no one wants to implement this secret.

When Shri Krishna had a headache, he asked for the feet of his devotees. But no one gave. People felt that give the dust of your feet to God! Sin will be incurred! We work with the mind throughout life. He thinks about knowledge. This is where the simplicity ends. Devotee and God, we small and he big. This idea starts working. By doing so they get caught in the web of sin, hell and ego and lose an opportunity. All are one for the Gopis. Where is the difference between Gopi and Krishna? Dust is also Krishna! In such a situation, what should be given to him and what should not be given? When the wise becomes available to the ultimate knowledge, he becomes silent. It becomes simple. As simple as I don't know anything. Simple and humble like Gopis.

If the attention is on ignorance, then man always remains humble and simple. The Gopis lack the wisdom of the mind. Because of this, they have less swagger. To become simple, Buddha did penance for six years, only after that he could forget the education and the knowledge gained from it. After twelve years of continuous silence and meditation, he became simple. Be speechless. Traveled from word to wordless. Consciousness can become vast, so it can become weightless. All this happened because of his ingenuity. Even Mahavir took years to cut the forest of theory, years were spent in making the inner mind vocal. Then the truth was revealed.

When a person's life is cooked in the sun, then only he becomes simple. As consciousness will expand in life. The sound of a Naad will appear within us. There will be a stagnation of beauty in the voice. It will become sweeter and simpler. There is no swara in kaccha and there is no pause in it. When the soil is cooked, then only rain water can be made into a receptacle. Otherwise, if it remains raw, there is a fear of melting with water. The day the completion of the construction will be achieved. On that day the person will become simple. A feeling of grace will prevail. There will be an appearance of a beauty, a grace and a simplicity. And then a stream of joy will start flowing inside.

To touch the stones is to touch a piece of the eternal. Praying in a way that at least the love of this evening, the longing of this dark hour will not pass away. Will survive among these ruins for years to come.

Nirmal Verma

Life is between two breaths

Life is between two breaths. Everything keeps changing in this life and will change. It is our delusion to consider hope as unchanging. No one is for anyone. Life comes, goes. Death is the truth of life. Everyone has accepted this universal truth. There is a saying, when it sees, the mind accepts. Till now he used to study in books and scriptures. Used to think about death. But when the mother passed away, I had to become aware of the bitter truth that if there is life, there is also death. Whether the mind accepts it or not. It does not matter. Second, its explanation is simply silent.

Just read a book - Sunset of Dwarka written by Dinkar Joshi. The last moments of Shri Krishna. If the world deviates from the rules and regulations of the universe, then time decides its destiny. This is the last sermon of Shri Krishna. God is injured by the fowler's arrow, the fowler is worried. Apologizes to the Lord. Shri Krishna says - material things have limits. The body also has a time limit. Every relationship has an inevitable end. It was Krishna's philosophy that if you accept every reality of life and its end with a natural sense, then there would be no sorrow.

Death is the end of life. There is a break in the infinite journey. If we say in the language of literature, then life is the climax of the drama. The end I am dialogue, acting. Death defines and interprets life most and decisively. I was distraught, delirious, so the Mahabharata came to my mind. It has a dialogue between Yaksha and Yudhishthira. This dialogue is famous. There is a question that what is the biggest surprise? Yudhishthir says - Death. It is in the light of this death that the entire Mahabharata reveals itself. Destruction i.e. Mahamrityu is made of the inner fabric – the story of Mahabharata. Death comes before the eyes as a tragedy. Death gives a message. Brings forth a vision.

Krishna's death, Bhishma's death, Karna's death, Pandavas' death, etc, etc. Every death tells a story. A narrative that is incomplete or unacceptable to the world. But whose story is his own. It is perfect for him. This is the reason why the Mahabharata remains a story of great sadness. I think life is also like Mahabharata. And everyone's story is complete for him and incomplete for others. Perhaps because of this I am also believing that mother's life was incomplete, but no it was complete. It is our vision which cannot be seen completely.

There is a unique world of death in Mahabharata. Death and destruction of all kinds. There is life, but it is also cursed. Ashwatthama's cursed immortality, Jarasandha, Kichak, Dushasana and Dhrishtadyumna's gruesome death. Krishna's Mahavirat Virag, then Duryodhan, Abhimanyu, Karna's Karun death. The burning of Kunti, Gandhari and Dhritarashtra in the forest fire is also an irony of the method, so is Vidura's death. Our life also suffers various forms of death. Or to say like this, it is cursedness, detachment and compassionate attachment. But he doesn't want to learn.

There are two characters in Mahabharata, who could not shed tears for anyone. One Bhishma and the other Shri Krishna. Even after destruction, he has a stable personality. Both are witness to the destruction of their dynasty. Can stop that destruction, but do not do so. Nietzsche has rightly said that some people are born after death. Probably right. The light of a person's life comes to the fore only after death. Not before that. Before that we do not do justice to life. That is why our sages and sages say in Upanishads and commentaries on philosophy that we should see the beginning of life from death.

Understand the philosophy of life in the light of death. The best to understand this philosophy is Harivansh Rai Bachchan's poem-

As far as I can see, the ocean of you waves

Someone dear standing on the other side, pulls us all.

We go today, tomorrow you go, don't know what will happen in the middle

You are on this side dear, we are there, don't know what will happen on the other side?

We are not like Ram, who forgets his sorrow in dignity and order. We are not even like Buddha, who talks about consciousness even in death, to which everyone is connected. We are not even like Bhishma and Krishna. We shed tears to forget the past. Forget yourself and walk at your own pace. While we do not know that time has its own speed, and its speed is circular. For this reason, the whole movement of life is circular in form of conch shell. That is why Indian life was called the cycle of life. From the smallest unit of time atom today, night, seasons, celestial constellations, planets, constellations, even the universe follows the cyclic motion. Similarly life too. Runs in circular motion. Birth, growth, childhood, youth, maturity, old age, death and rebirth. Circular motion. But what does one see? To man, to his speed. Not the time that sets it in motion. Because of this, everything seems to be developing linearly. While it is not the speed of time, it is the mobility of human beings. The attainment of death can be a turning point or a turning point in the dynamics of a human being. For a new development. But for time it is a continuous journey.

In whose heart his beloved resides, then he forgets himself and calls out to the beloved. When the sound of the beloved starts resonating in Rome, then there is no desire for any external melody or rhythm and he spontaneously starts dancing drowning in the joy of meeting.

Bulleshah

The search for happiness in life is the search for life itself

What is happiness in this material world? Happiness of family, happiness of wife, children, brothers and brothers and happiness of mother and father! The pleasure of living in the world, the pleasure of enjoying it! What does a man not do throughout his life? Throughout life there is running, fighting, and upheaval and then knowledge comes. But it doesn't matter anymore. This is not my story, this is the story of most of the world. The pursuit of happiness in this life is the pursuit of life itself. It is written in the Mahabharata that whether it is happiness or sorrow, whether it is dear or unpleasant, whatever you get, accept it as if it is Prasad. Never give up in your mind. Happiness and sorrow, defeat and victory - is this duality? Of life. And both break somewhere, happiness breaks with pride, sadness breaks with inferiority.

The biggest truth of life is life itself. On this earth, this ultimate truth has to be realized by everyone – through struggle, through love, on the path of action and devotion. In search of self and seeking ultimate happiness, the search for truth goes on throughout life. It is the movement of life itself, the struggle. Whether we like it or not, we are in motion. Now it depends on us to make this speed relative to nature. Take your life towards the goal i.e. the core. There is movement in the whole universe. The whole universe is in motion. The Moon relative to the Earth, then the Earth is moving aiming at the Sun. Earth has to face so much struggle in this sequence – eclipse, scorching heat, drought, meteorite fall, earthquake, and volcano. But the earth does not give up. Litterateur Nirmal Verma writes in his novel *Aakhali Aranya* that when this great knowledge comes to our mind and heart, it is too late... then man is not capable of it! He doesn't take happiness with his tongs, he comes to pick up her ashes....

Man is insignificant and insignificant in the vastness of space and time. My mother understood this more than me. That's why before every important and secondary work, we were taught to bow down before that great power. When the goal is big, dedicate yourself. In front of that vastness. Dedication is an important formula in moving forward in life, through which a person makes the goal easy. That is, there is only one truth, speed. No pause and no rest. This is the message of nature. Speed means travel. Life journey All living beings in nature have a journey of life. Mai's life was also a journey. On May 17, 2012, when the words stopped, his life also stopped. As time went on, she also went on a great journey together. After a long journey of life, when words became silent, life itself became a squid. What did you gain and what did you lose in this journey? This feeling started rising in my mind. I remember the words of Isaac Asimov. He has said that - Life is pleasant and death is calm. The transition between it is the one that is painful. Okay. As long as the mother was there, life was pleasant. Quiet now. The word does not matter, because the word also has an identity, its sweetness is related to the person and the moment. If that is not sweetness, then there is no identity. So words are meaningless.

Nothing can be greater than a mother and her affection, this is a universal truth. How can we repay the one who kept us in the womb for nine months, nourished us with blood and compassion, kept us in our arms for years and held us close to our heart for life? The day he died Worrying about son more than himself. On the edge of death. Recently I had read a book - Who will cry on your death. Crying is not just because someone was yours. Crying, therefore, was understood as a philosophy of life, in its own simple and easy language. The truth of a life was told, to understand which man runs away.

When one touch is heavy on countless words. When one lap becomes bigger than infinite happiness. When a gesture removes infinite confusions and a face, which answers innumerable questions. She is only a mother. When he was in dire straits, wandering from door to door in search of a job, it was his mother who had borrowed money from his father and put on an emerald ring. It was the mother who used to be more worried and restless than me on the birth of my daughters. There is no one else except my mother, who is unable to get up due to ill health, and puts the plate on the dining table before I leave for office. And that too was the love of mother, who used to keep some money saved from father and sweets in my mouth while I was going out or when I left the house till death. I used to say - now you can do all this, Taru. She silenced me by replying – keep it. Come on, come in handy. I have been working for 20 years, but there is always a shortage. This is the happiness of the family.

There is an Arabic saying that God is not everywhere, so he created mother. When the man asked the Prophet, who is the most respected? Got the answer, mother... And then? The Prophet again said, Mother.... And after that the answer was still the same, Mother.... I see where in our happiness do we find happiness and joy? Where is the joy of life when you are not your own to share happiness? Who will tell about these moments of happiness? Walter Benjamin, writing on Proust, said that none of us had time to live out the real dramas of our lives, which were written in our destiny. This is what makes us old – only this, nothing else. The wrinkles and creases of our faces indicate the great manias, addictions and introverts who came to visit us and we were not at home.

The best and most beautiful things in the world cannot be seen, they cannot even be touched. They have to be felt from the heart.

Helen Keller

Sarvamangalam will come true, with all-embracing

Integration with the creation, self-awakening (consciousness development) and mutual cooperation are the indicators of the movement of the individual, society and the state. The basis of the life of the creature - Prana i.e. oxygen - is received from the plants, and the plants get their life - i.e. carbon dioxide from the animal world. It is because of this mutual complementarity that the world is running and only on this thought-philosophy development of the state is possible and man will be able to move forward. The path of humanism will now pass through Sarvatism i.e. welfare of all. The same consciousness is there in all the living beings of this creation, if we can develop the religion of sacrifice and service with cooperation and love from it, then only welfare will happen. In animism, each individual will care for himself as well as all individuals, all living entities will move forward connecting with each other.

What is animism? It literally means that there is only one soul within everyone. When there is no antagonism or disparity among the creatures of this world on the basis of the soul, then there should not be any such feeling in enjoyment and profit. Means everyone should get what I want. The way the Lord who resides within me remains happy, we have to be prepared for the happiness of the Lord who resides within everyone. Because it is not fundamentally a division. We need bread, cloth, house and Arogya or inner peace. This should be the equal right of all, because the same God resides within everyone. "You are one in the whole world, Shri Hari" in the society Snatching won't do. We should see our own happiness and keep increasing our happiness by snatching the happiness of others, this Canalise is the sign of that society, in which there is dominance of isolation, superiority and discrimination. But due to the change in the ideal, today the aim of the entire society has been limited to enjoyment and that too for itself. Be it any field, the talk or work of building society and individual has reached a low level.

In such a situation, from where will the system or policy be able to give any result? This is also happening because the criterion of difference between a person and a person is made on material factors, money, power and intellectuality, and on the same basis itself is claimed to be superior and hence its right to more enjoyment and benefits. Therefore, it is natural that in a society where there is devotion to spiritualism, a person himself will give up those facilities which are not available to all. Enjoying delicious dishes among the hungry and living in luxurious houses in huts cannot be called justified from anywhere. When the discipline of good thoughts spreads, then equality and harmony become the voice of our heart and change the way of living.

It has been told in Indian life that man lives life at four levels. Body, mind, intellect and soul. When a man lives life at the level of the body, that means he is always concerned about enjoyment and material things. Such a man cannot be separated from animal. By living life at the level of the body, a person has been reduced to competition and the race to get ahead of others. In this situation, each person has his own happiness and his own sorrow. Which is different from the other. Earlier, the happiness of one person used to be the happiness of the whole family and the sorrows were also shared by the whole family together. We used to easily aggregate the sentiment as well. Now a person has his own goal, which keeps him away from family and society. Has its own priority, which makes the relationship uncomfortable. And beyond this the ego of each individual. Now our house has become a structure of gross and inert feelings and substances.

My happiness is within me. The search for peace lies within me. There is no end to desires and aspirations, so running after them means searching for a mirage. The desire for material things and comforts is not bad. It is not bad to run away till an essential need provided the communication and relationship with the family, society and self does not deteriorate. Society will be benefited only by the relation of man with the world-nature in a sattvic co-life. In this indulgent time everything is for indulgence. And man has been created for its enjoyment. In the present system and thinking, there is no symbiotic relationship between man with his nature and the global system. Everything in this world is not for human enjoyment. This thing has to be understood. If all the components of nature are meant for man to enjoy, then will anyone enjoy man too? It has to be accepted. This enjoyment will be done by nature itself through its dreadful destruction. I.e. through flood, drought, earthquake, tsunami, volcano. It is not a sign of superiority to establish dominance over the nature which is weaker than itself.

The sign of superiority and greater development is that we establish harmony with all living beings and walk in a symbiotic relationship. The boon that man has received from the universal nature is not just vegetation, water, mineral wealth and sky. Man's relationship with cosmic nature is spiritual. The core is the conscious correlation. That's why it was said that what is in the soul, is in the divine. That's why all the products of this nature should be taken as Prasad. Food, water, light, air, greenery, coolness etc. all should be obtained like an akinchan (Being vacant person). At the same time, it is the main characteristic of a human being to make a relation with this variable nature with his soul. This is a spontaneous action and through this the journey of development can continue unabated.

That's why one should not limit his life only to himself. It has to connect with its family, society, village, country and the world. It should be the nature of man to connect his life with the larger life around him, as well as to experience the oneness of symbiosis. With this nature, man should create an auspicious combination with the world or nature outside himself, so that man can experience the greater and the infinite in himself. This will not happen by enjoyment. If this were so, then Buddha would not have to leave the house to search. It is neither concerned with wealth nor with lack. You just need to have the right understanding. For this one has to move beyond the physical level. When there is co-relation with the world-nature or there is an interview with oneself, then there is no difference between Tathagat and Kabir.

Only after knowing oneself, a person is able to do the right thing with all his knowledge and thinking. He feels unity around him. After this whatever he does is the best and its results are also unlimited. Both his will and his goal are included in the divine providence.

Maharishi Arvind

Spirituality means a life of balance

What is the meaning of spirituality? Balanced life. Life speed in totality. Successful life if all these are included in one sentence, then it would mean that if we give paramount place to the Supreme Soul in life, then we are spiritual. What is this supreme soul? This world is one with the variable creatures. We do not have control over the events of life. But we can have a stand on such incidents. Let us look at each and every event and thing in terms of whether it takes us closer to God or to perfection or not? Due to such karma, do we have a sensory connection with all the components of nature or not? If it does, then we are spiritual, not otherwise.

Behind the search for spirituality is a constant desire for depth in our lives. Contemplation, meditation, prayer, exercise, entertainment and realization of devotion to God etc. have the power to illuminate the life force hidden in the depths of the human mind. If we are spiritual then we will respect all life. No discrimination. Everyone's respect. Of life of creation where life originates from. Where life flourishes. And spreads. Whether in plants, birds or humans. This is a positive thought. We suffer when we think of the entire creation only with the body or intellect. Give trouble to others. We always have to increase the tendency to see our thoughts from the third level of existence i.e. from the heart. Listen with your heart and decide. Your neighbour's heart is also beating. It has to be understood that the tree which is in the field, the stream of life is also flowing in it. This earth that is, it is also breathing. Whether it is a small insect or a big animal or a bird, the same life is manifesting in everyone on this earth. So why don't we respect it from the heart? Existence is every moment. But we have made ourselves stand under the cover of material happiness. This is not spirituality.

We become non-spiritual when we separate ourselves from nature. Then we do not see any interest in blooming flowers. There is no sense in serving a poor person. At the time of praising others, the heart closes its doors. But we take great pleasure in blasphemy, in violence. Osho has presented this attitude very beautifully – Meditate on yourself. When you are expressing sorrow in someone's sorrow, close your eyes for a moment and see if the juice is not coming. Are you not feeling good, are you not enjoying sympathy? If you are enjoying, then consider it as fun or disease. And when someone appears happy, do you get jealous? Does it happen that when the other person is happy, you feel pain? If there is suffering, then you do not have respect for life. Wherever life blossoms and there is happiness, then we should be happy.

All unbalanced situations in this world take us away from ourselves. To go away from oneself means to become non-spiritual. Starting with the body, whether it is overeating or undereating. Both situations take us away from ourselves, where there is sickness, not health. People say that the search for God is the basic spirituality. Even if it is accepted, then how can this search be done only for its own interest?

When we are complete, then only we will be spiritual. For this consciousness has to be expanded. How to develop and expand consciousness? The first thing to do is to reject everything that follows. Refuse to express everything that drags us down. This rejection should not be expressed only at the level of actions, but also at the level of thoughts and feelings. If such a habit is formed, then the inner aspiration towards the beloved thing decreases and the consciousness does not go into a downward state. After this the question arises that how to make the consciousness vast? The easiest way is to associate ourselves with the vast or the infinite. Like the depth of the ocean or the boundless expanse of the sky. When we put ourselves in the limit of such infinite and infinite, then the consciousness also becomes one with the infinite. If the individual's consciousness is connected to a higher plane, then the personality will also be expansive. An example. This was the reaction of many friends after reading Tagore's Gitanjali. I did not understand. Is not clear. I had replied to him that do not make the mistake of considering Gitanjali as a poem. It is not a poem but a song. Poetry written in identification with existence. In which there is the prayer of that infinite. When a person becomes so huge or makes himself huge. Only then there will be welfare of this material world.

There are many difficulties in the path of spirituality. The first is not to adopt it in totality. We accept or adopt it piece by piece. Research on the role of spirituality in health benefits is increasing these days. The Harvard Medical School of Continuing Education offers a course called Spirituality and Healing in Medicine. The course brings together theologians and physicians from around the world to discuss the role of spirituality in the treatment of illness and pain. While this research may be new regarding the use of spirituality for healing, it is not a new concept. Spirituality was adopted in every sphere of ancient Indian life.

The idea of anything in pieces, binds the boundaries. This increases tension. Whereas perfection on the other hand accepts everything. Does not discard anything, but puts everything in its proper place. The way to make life complete, that is, to make it spiritual, is to see things in totality. For this, it is necessary to see life, the events of life, everything or things happening from a great height so that its totality can be realized. Whatever was before, whatever is now and whatever will be. All these things have to be seen or experienced together. Only then will we feel immense joy in seeing or knowing the eternally living.

What is the pursuit of perfection? There is a traditional story. A craftsman reluctantly put down his hammer and chisel and went to see who had come to see me in the studio so late at night. On opening the door, he saw an acquaintance of his standing waiting for him in the full moon's moonlight. Used to be. Shilpi greeted him silently and returned to his workplace. His friend also followed him. He said, we have not seen you for many days. You are still not engaged in the construction of that idol, are you? Without giving any answer to his question, the craftsman took his friend to the masterpiece he had labored for months to create. His friend became silent after seeing that artwork. At last he said softly, never before had you carved such a grand expression of the human spirit. This is the best work of yours so far. Shilpi said that, I think when it will be completed, then it will be as you are thinking. But I still have a lot of work to do on this. His outfit doesn't look right - this muscle needs to be fleshed out a bit more and the countenance needs to be softened a bit more. But all these are small things. Friend said. Turning to his friend, the craftsman said, it is these small things that give perfection, and perfection is no small thing.

There is a correlation between spirituality and freedom. Freedom is a natural demand of a person for the overall development of life. In its essence it is the complete realization of the highest consciousness. It is an expression of oneness and union with God. Its complete link can be expressed with love. In the state of love, a person becomes occupied with service and self-sacrifice. Complete freedom is attained only when one becomes completely one with the Supreme, because all ignorance, unconsciousness is bondage. It makes a person powerless, limited and incapable. Even a small fraction of ignorance within oneself brings a sense of limitation in a person. Then the person cannot remain free. As long as there is a sense of unconsciousness in the being, it is a bondage. Only by attaining complete unity with the Supreme Being can there be complete freedom.

Only a spiritual person can be free from all bondages. Or only a free person can be spiritual. There is no external influence on such a person and he himself determines his actions and its fruits. On the other hand, even a free person becomes spiritual when he is under self. In both these situations, a person needs to see and know his constantly arising impulses and emotions. Life is revealed only when we go into the depths of our being. In Indian life, Mahatma Buddha made life spiritual through freedom of self. On the other hand, Mahatma Gandhi brought freedom to the common people in public life on the basis of spirituality. Consider - the situation was completely opposite in both the periods. One freed himself by renouncing worldly life, then talked about spiritual contemplation in practice. The second proclaimed freedom in public life through spirituality while living a worldly life. Be it Buddha or Gandhi. The scientific experiment of spirituality and freedom of these people continued throughout their life. These two sages are timeless in Indian thought, who got free from all bondages and became successful on the basis of their deeds. His specialty was also that he did not get inspiration or strength from anywhere else for his success. Both rejected established beliefs and expanded consciousness through their higher intelligence, wisdom and intuition. Apart from traditions and rooted principles, he thought and paved the way for contemplation and action.

Spirituality is actually the complete realization and expression of this multidimensional human life. For this, easy and simple and sensitive methods of conduct and behaviour are searched in every era. Scientific research is done for this. Mahatma Buddha gave a scientific vision of an eightfold path to spirituality of life. So Mahatma Gandhi did truth and non-violence. Purity of the means to achieve the goal. One who transcends the world? He is able to accept life as a whole. He hears and accepts the existence beyond what is seen in this world. Only he succeeds. This thing is completely true on Mahatma Gandhi and Mahatma Buddha. Both the great men encroached on the world. In this century Maharishi Arvind, Raman Maharshi, Ramakrishna Paramhans, Tagore, Jagdishchandra Basu etc. some tried to make this world more sensitive by encroaching on the world.

The present age accepts spirituality, but at the same time adds scientific words to it. Scientific Spirituality. Spirituality is scientific in itself. If the meaning of scientific outlook is to negate prejudices, idiocy and wrong beliefs and to promote reasonable, truth-seeking and purposeful investigation, then either Mahatma Buddha or Gandhi both thought from a scientific point of view. Both made public life sensitive by giving importance to discretion and consciousness. Serious spiritual scientific experiments on spirituality were done in India only. Whereas in the West, spiritual inquiries have been limited to philosophical thinking. It has been said in the Taittiriya Upanishad that science alone increases the sacrifices and deeds. All the deities worship science in the supreme form of Brahman. Those who know science in the form of Brahman, engage in the same kind of contemplation, they attain fulfilment of all desires by being freed from sins through this body.

Eminent psychologist Carl Jung discussed spiritualism with Paramana Maharishi when his the paranoia ended with Freud. Carl Jung used to believe that there is an invisible unconscious hand behind conscious behaviour, but because of Freud's acceptance of lust and its suppression as everything, Jung came in contact with the Indian mystic. Later he wrote on his behalf in the foreword to Sri Raman and His Message to Modern Man that Sri Raman is the beacon of scientific expression of spirituality. Ramana Maharshi, discussing scientific spirituality, said that its basic elements are five. Curiosity to the first which is called research problem. Second, according to the nature and situation, the selection of the right method means research method. Thirdly, impeccable spiritual practice done in the disorder less laboratory of the body and mind. In scientific language, it is an experiment done in a controlled situation, in which continuous survey is done. Fourthly, testing and continuous assessment of the experiment being done in a certain order and the final result of all these means proper conclusion.

The eightfold path and fundamental ideas like truth and non-violence came to the society only after serious spiritual experiments. In the ancient Vedic period, the female sage Vishvavara gave the idea of Karma theory. With the inspiration of Goddess Anasuiya, after practicing the theory of Karma, he said that the effects of actions are immediate, while the effects of Karma last for many births. There is no coincidence of any kind of desire and resolution in action. They end up giving an immediate effect. Human vagina is not affected by this action. From insects to insects and birds come in this. Karma principle works in human life. Karma is not only what we do, but it is done in the form of thought, desire and emotion simultaneously on both the matter and the conscious plane. Yagya theory of Maharishi Yajnavalkya and Maharishi Vishwamitra and the use of Gayatri Mahamantra were discussed a lot in Indian thought, but there was less discussion about the marriage rules based on the alliance between man and woman of Vishvavara and Vedic woman sage Surya Savitri. Scientific research on spirituality continues continuously through Mahavira's Syadvad, Panini's Yoga Sutras, Swami Vivekananda's Navya Vedanta, Rabindranath Tagore's Naturalism, Maharishi Aurobindo's construction of supermind etc. in modern times.

Reference Books :

1. Akhand Jyoti: Carl Jung found realization in the company of Raman Maharshi, July 2009 and page-14.
2. Shree Maa: Suryalokit Path: Publisher - Sri Arvind Society, Pondicherry, 1993 and page-208

3. Osho: Ishopanishad, Hind Pocket Books, New Delhi.

4. Taitriya Upanishad, Brahmananda Valli - 5/1

5. Chopra, Dr. Deepak: Seven Spiritual Laws of Success, Full Circle, 2003 and page-32.

6. Tuldharia, Badrisah: Daishik Shastra, Deendayal Upadhyay Prakashan, First Edition 2002, page 03.

7. Harivansh: Good Family, Better Nation, Prabhat Khabar Sunday, January 18, 2009 and page-08.

8. Sahay, Rajalakshmi: Terrorist mushrooms growing on the curb of social concern, Prabhat Khabar 19 November 2008 and page-02.

9. Krishnaswamy, OR: The Wisdom of Thiruvallar, Introduction to a Guide to Living Commentary, Bharatiya Vidya Bhavan, 2004.

10. Ranganathananda, Swami: Democratic Administration in the Light of Pragmatic Vedanta, Ramakrishna Math, Nagpur 2001 and page-70.

11. Thengadi, Dattopant: Chintan Patheya, Jagruti Prakashan", Noida 1990, page-33 and 34.

12. Agnya: The tree standing in the open, Vagdevi Publications, 1999 page-165.

13. Osho: An Eternal Journey to India, Diamond Pocket Books

14. Ranganathananda, Swami: Democratic Administration in the Light of Pragmatic Vedanta, Ramakrishna Math, Nagpur 2001 and page-70.

15. Paramahansa Yogananda: Man's Eternal Quest, Yogoda Satsang Society.

16. Swami Ranganathananda: The Message of the Upanishads, Publishers Swami Brahmasthananda Editions 2005.

17. Pramahansayogananda: Man's Continuing Quest, Jayco Publications, 2010.

18. Tik Nyat Hanh: Jahan Jahan Charan Pare Gautam K, Hind Pocket Books 1998.

19. Osho: Ek Onkar Satnam, Diamond Pocket Books, Edition 1998.

Damyank Murari currently Senior Deputy General Manager (Public Relations) at Usha Martin andCSR) at Ranchi, Jharkhand. He can be contacted at e-mail- unantantpanunlanda/humpsnbwu and mobile 9934320630.